WITHDRAWN

Chicago's great world's fairs

general editor
Paul Greenhalgh

Chicago's great world's fairs

John E. Findling

MANCHESTER UNIVERSITY PRESS
Manchester and New York

distributed exclusively in the USA and Canada by St Martin's Press

Published by Manchester University Press
Oxford Road, Manchester M13 9NR, UK
and Room 400, 175 Fifth Avenue, New York, NY 10010, USA

Distributed exclusively in the USA and Canada
by St. Martin's Press, Inc., 175 Fifth Avenue, New York,
NY 10010, USA

British Library Cataloguing-in-Publication Data

A catalogue record for this book is available from the British
Library

Library of Congress Cataloging-in-Publication Data

Findling, John E.
    Chicago's great world's fairs / John E. Findling.
        p.   cm. — (Studies in design and material culture)
    Includes bibliographical references.
    ISBN 0–7190–3630–5
    1. Century of Progress International Exposition (1933–1934 :
Chicago, Ill.)—HIstory.   2. World's Columbian Exposition (1893 :
Chicago, Ill.)—History.   I. Title.   II. Series.
T501.B1F56   1994
907.4′773′11—dc20

                                                            93–49015

ISBN 0 7190 3630 5 *hardback*

Printed in Great Britain
by Redwood Books, Trowbridge

Contents

Figures

Sources

Fig. 1: Wolfgang Friebe, *Buildings of the World's Fairs*, Leipzig, 1985

Figs 2–7, 9–13: *Official Views of the World's Columbian Exposition*, Chicago, 1893

Fig. 8: F. Dundas Todd et al., *World's Fair Through a Camera*, St Louis, 1893

Fig. 27: Postcard, *A Century of Progress International Exposition*, Chicago, 1934

Figs 15, 17, 19–22, 25, 28: *Official Guide Book of the Fair*, Chicago, 1933

Fig. 14: Author

Figs 16, 18, 23, 24, 26, 29: *Official View Book: A Century of Progress Exposition*, Chicago, 1933

General editor's foreword

The history of design and material cultural study can include within its brief the examination of events as well as objects. Certain types of event are vital for the dissemination of objects and information to their publics. Principal amongst these are the international exhibitions held periodically around the world after 1850. Variously known as Great Exhibitions, Expositions Universelles, World's Fairs, and, more recently, Expo's, these exhibitions have been amongst the most extravagant cultural enterprises ever staged. Fortunes were spent on the erection of cities of temporary buildings, which would be filled with products of all kinds, from everywhere.

Despite having a philanthropic rationale in the charting of the past and future course of civilization, the international exhibitions came to acquire such a political and material potency by the turn of the twentieth century that their status and success was often guaranteed. By the 1930s, nations which ignored or scorned international exhibitions took risks not only with their cultural status, but also with their national economy.

Chicago has played an important role in the history of exhibitions. The city's first World's Fair, of 1893, was one of the most lavish of the nineteenth century. It contributed new exhibition techniques to the genre, as well as permanently establishing the status of Chicago. Having struggled with other American cities for the right to hold the Fair, after the Columbian Exposition closed, it counted only New York as a serious rival.

The city's second Fair, of 1933/4, was also dramatically successful, demonstrating not only an impressive industrial wealth, but also the extent to which the cultural hegemony was moving from Europe towards America. Chicago appeared to be more able to explore such concepts as 'modernity' than most of her European counterparts.

If the first exhibition confirmed the arrival of America on the world stage, the second revealed its leadership of the Western nations.

Preface and acknowledgements

In 1893 and again in 1933–34, the midwestern city of Chicago hosted world's fairs that contributed significantly to the history of architecture and design in America. These two fairs, the World's Columbian Exposition and the Century of Progress Exposition, also reflected in the manner and style of their exhibits the state of material culture in the United States at the times they were staged. As a topic of serious historical inquiry, world's fairs have attracted scholars for only a relatively short time, although in the last twenty years, the study of fairs has generated an increasing amount of interest and resulted in a number of note-worthy publications. Several of those publications have dealt with the World's Columbian Exposition, but none has focused on the later Chicago fair, the Century of Progress. For that reason, readers will find that the major portion of this book deals with the Century of Progress, its architecture, and its exhibits and concessions.

My interest in world's fairs as a research topic stems from a seminar I taught at Indiana University Southeast in 1982, when I first learned of the paucity of resources on fairs. That led me to edit, with Kim Pelle, a reference work, *Historical Dictionary of World's Fairs and Expositions, 1851–1988* (1990), to which I contributed the essay on the Century of Progress. That essay, in turn, led to this present work on the Chicago fairs.

A number of institutions and individuals have helped along the way on this project, and they deserve public thanks. Paul Greenhalgh of the Victoria and Albert Museum, London, the series editor, invited me to contribute to the series. The archives staff at the University of Illinois at Chicago, where the records of the Century of Progress are housed, were both helpful and patient with my many requests for documents relating to the fair, as were librarians at the Chicago Historical Society, the Art Institute of Chicago, Indiana University at Bloomington, and the National Archives in Washington D.C. Special thanks go to the graduate students, faculty, and staff of the Winterthur Institute, Winterthur, Delaware, and particularly Kristin Herron, for helping me understand the nature of material culture better.

As always, the library staff at Indiana University Southeast were of great assistance in facilitating interlibrary loan requests, dealing with research queries, and smiling a lot. An Intercampus Scholar grant from Indiana University and a sabbatical leave from Indiana University Southeast were important in providing

Preface and acknowledgements

me with additional time (and space) to work on this project. Thanks to Kathy Theilen, who, I hope, learned much by helping me with the research and reading and commenting on the manuscript. Betty Riggs also helped with some of the research and Kim Pelle and my wife Carol also gave perceptive readings to the manuscript and helped with the indexing. I am grateful to the staff at Manchester University Press, especially Jane Hammond Foster, Hannah Freeman, and Susanne Atkin, for their gracious help in working with the typescript. I am grateful to my parents and to my good friend, George Vician, for sharing their recollections of the Century of Progress Exposition with me. Finally, since I inflicted this topic on my students for a 1991 seminar and they endured it with grace and good humor, and taught me much in the process, this book is dedicated to them.

1   Chicago: the host city

To describe Chicago, one would need all the superlatives set in a row. Grandest, flattest, – muddiest, dustiest, – hottest, coldest, – wettest, driest[1]

The area that is now Chicago first attracted attention in the seventeenth century, when travelers discovered that it was a relatively short portage between Lake Michigan and the Des Plaines River, which flows into the Illinois River, which in turn flows into the Mississippi River. As the Chicago portage was on a route commonly used by French explorers and Indians, traders settled there from time to time, and a mission operated for a few years, although no one saw much potential in the flat, swampy land. During the early eighteenth century, there was almost constant turmoil between the French trappers and explorers and the Indians, and eventually whites simply avoided the area.[2]

The Treaty of Paris (1763) transferred the area to British control, and when the newly independent United States created the Northwest Territory in 1787, American settlers began to arrive from the east. A consequence of this was warfare between the Indians and American troops in the 1790s, ended by the Treaty of Greenville (1795). In that treaty, the Indians ceded a parcel of land 'at the mouth of the Chikago River' to the United States as the site for a military fort. In 1803, Fort Dearborn, named in honor of Henry Dearborn, President Thomas Jefferson's secretary of war, was built.

A number of settlers came to the area near the fort, and for about ten years, there was an uneasy truce with the Indians. All of this changed in August 1812, after the outbreak of the War of 1812. At that time, the Indians, loosely allied with the British, attacked about 100 Americans, including some thirty women and children, as they attempted to evacuate Fort Dearborn. Nearly all were killed and the fort was burned to the ground.[3]

In 1817, a second Fort Dearborn was completed, more settlers arrived, and the Indians were gradually pushed out of the area. Illinois became a state in 1818, and the military left Fort Dearborn in 1823; it became a kind of campground for travelers passing through on their way west. The final treaty with the Indians followed the short Blackhawk War of 1832–33.

Chicago was surveyed and plotted on the order of the Illinois state legislature in 1829 and incorporated as a town in August 1833 and as a city in 1837. Lured, perhaps, by stories of the rich land and agreeable climate related by veterans of the Blackhawk War as well as by talk of a canal connecting the lake and the river, settlers came in significant numbers after 1833. Canal construction began in 1836, and by 1837 Chicago was the largest city in Illinois with a population of 4,718.

Chicago's growth (and the construction of the canal) was slowed by the nationwide depression of 1837–41, but later in the 1840s, the city resumed its development as a regional commercial center, attracting national attention in 1847 by hosting the River and Harbor Convention. This convention attracted 3,000 delegates and national press attention over the issue of federally-sponsored river and harbor improvements in the wake of President James K. Polk's veto of a bill that would have authorized such projects. The publicity generated by this convention was important in bringing more business and people to Chicago and in hastening the completion of the canal and the arrival of the railroad, both of which occurred the following year. More than anything else, the railroad keyed Chicago's development into the most important city of the Midwest, surpassing Cincinnati and St Louis.[4]

By 1870, Chicago boasted a population of 334,270 and was the busiest railroad center in the entire country. Immigrants provided a ready labor supply for new enterprises in meat packing, iron, lumber, and transportation. Under the guidance of a wealthy merchant, Potter Palmer, State Street emerged as a stylish, mile-long retail and hotel thoroughfare with the eight-story, 225 room Palmer House hotel as its centerpiece. No one could have foreseen that the great heart of the city, its buildings hastily built of wood during the years of rapid expansion, would be utterly destroyed by fire in less than twenty-four hours.[5]

The Chicago fire broke out on 8 October 1871 at the corner of Jefferson and DeKoven Streets, southwest of the central business district. A summer drought had dried out the wooden buildings, and a wind from the southwest pushed the fire north and east through downtown Chicago, across the Chicago River (which many believed would stop the fire), and into the north side, where the next day it burned itself out in Lincoln Park, then a rather barren place. Over 300 persons were killed in the fire, some 100,000 were left homeless, and 17,000 buildings were destroyed. The total property damage was estimated at $88 million.[6]

The city, however, recovered quickly. Some businesses were functioning again within 48 hours, relief supplies arrived from all parts of the country, and a genuine spirit of civic boosterism developed almost overnight, echoed in the phrase, 'Chicago Shall Rise Again!' Out of the ashes, too, arose the notion that the fire was a seminal event in the city's history, and all future histories of modern Chicago would start with the fire and its heroic aftermath.

Chicago promoters went to eastern cities like New York and successfully touted the investment potential of rebuilding their city, and new buildings soon began to rise from the ashes of the old. Young architects, attracted by the opportunity to design a city practically from scratch, came to Chicago and made it into the center of architectural and engineering innovation for the next generation. Several of them went to work for William LeBaron Jenney, a Civil War demolition specialist who came to Chicago after the war and in the 1880s, pioneered the use of steel frame construction for commercial buildings. Among those who worked for Jenney were Louis Sullivan, who would become known as the 'father of the skyscraper,' and William Holabird and Martin Roche, who established a partnership in 1881 that became one of the leading architectural firms in the city for over forty years. Another protégé of Jenney's was Daniel H. Burnham, who came to Chicago as a boy in the 1850s, served apprenticeships with Jenney and other Chicago architects, and in 1873, formed a partnership with John W. Root, a New York architect who had come to Chicago after the fire. By the 1890s, Burnham & Root was the leading architectural practice in the city, and its central role in the World's Columbian Exposition was testimony to its influence. Because of steel frame construction, the practicality of the elevator, the rapid growth of Chicago and the constraints of its urban geography, many of the new buildings the new generation of Chicago architects designed were larger, more stylish, and more efficient than their predecessors, and they all met the new building code and fire regulations that the city government adopted in the wake of the disaster.[7]

Only two years after the devastating fire, Chicago hosted a significant exposition in a large building constructed on the lakefront near the downtown area. Known as the Chicago Interstate Industrial Exposition, this fair had its origins in the creation of the Northwestern Mechanical and Agricultural Association in 1869. Founders of that organization planned a fair, but the fire set them back. In June 1872, John B. Drake, George S. Bowen, and John Irving Pearce obtained a license to form a corporation that would establish a permanent industrial fair, but they were unable to capitalize the venture. In February 1873, serious planning, under the leadership of Potter Palmer, Marshall Field, and other influential Chicagoans, began for a fair that would open on 15 September and last for at least four weeks. Organizers sold more than $75,000 worth of shares at $100 each by 20 March, and planning began for an exposition building.

The eminent architect William W. Boyington designed the 800 foot by 260 foot building, which was situated on the lakefront between Monroe Street and Jackson Street. An executive committee, headed by Palmer and including Joseph Medill, W. F. Coolbaugh, Jacob Rosenberg, N. K. Fairbank, and C. B. Farwell, had to raise an extra $100,000 to cover all the costs of the building. Construction began 20 June 1873 with piles driven into the soft soil near the lake. The fair building reflected the architecture typical of exhibition buildings of the time; it was a large Italianate greenhouse, with brick walls and an elliptical glass roof supported on giant trusses with a 150-foot span. The hall had some 232,800 square feet of floor space, with a central dome 60 feet in diameter and 165 feet high and smaller domes at either end that were 48 feet square and 140 feet high. The building took just ninety days to construct.

The exposition opened 25 September 1873 and closed 12 November 1873, and attracted about 60,000 visitors. About 580 businesses and organizations exhibited, placing their wares in one of eight departments or categories which ranged from Household and Personal Objects to Natural History, a taxonomy typical for fairs of that era. In addition, there was a fine arts show, highlighted by an Albert Bierstadt painting of the sierra in southern California and a number of works by European artists. Most of the businesses and artists who exhibited, however, were from the Chicago area.

The executive committee called a stockholder's meeting for 23 December 1873 to discuss future plans, including enlarging the building and devoting any future profits to the establishment of some kind of civic institution, such as a polytechnic school or a permanent industrial fair. The Chicago Interstate Industrial Exposition continued to hold annual exhibitions for the next eighteen years, at which time the building was demolished to make way for the Art Institute.[8]

The Chicago Interstate Industrial Exposition was only the first sign of the tremendous progress Chicago was to make in the years between the fire and the World's Columbian Exposition of 1893. As the city expanded through annexation and attracted more than its share of the thousands of immigrants coming to the United States from Europe during those years, its population grew from well under 400,000 to over 1.2 million. This growth was not without its problems, however. Poverty, political corruption, radical labor agitation, and a high level of crime were social consequences of the rapid growth and contributed to a sense, held particularly by New Yorkers and other easterners, that Chicago was little more than an overgrown frontier town.[9]

The period was marked by a rapid rise in industrial activity, carried on in factories that spewed thick black smoke (one reason that the city itself was called the 'Black City' in contrast to the World's Columbian Exposition's appellation, the 'White City'). Reid Badger quotes an Italian visitor to Chicago, '[D]uring my stay of one week, I did not see in Chicago anything but darkness: smoke, clouds dirt, and an extraordinary number of sad and grieved persons.'[10]

Many of these 'sad and grieved' individuals tried to alleviate their problems through participation in the labor movement of the Gilded Age.[11] By the 1880s, this movement had become strongly influenced by anarchists, who doubted that any form of government could or should function on behalf of the people. Organized labor was perceived as a threat by the general public, and workers were often brutally treated by police or professional strikebreakers whenever they tried to express their grievances by means of a public rally or work stoppage. The climactic event was the Haymarket Riot on 4 May 1886, when a bomb thrown by an unknown person killed seven policemen as they tried to disperse a crowd of workers at the Haymarket, an open square on the city's west side.

Eight anarchists were tried and convicted on charges of murder, despite the lack of evidence against them. Four were hanged, one committed suicide, and three were pardoned in 1893 by Governor John Altgeld. The incident was a major blow both to the labor movement and to Chicago's reputation, but on the other hand, it may have brought to Chicago's wealthy a heightened sense of social and civic responsibility, evidenced by a rise in philanthropic and reform-minded activities. Thus the 1890s witnessed a flowering of museums, art galleries, educational institutions, and libraries, as well as the development of the social settlement movement, designed to improve life for the poor and downtrodden. The keystone of this movement, Hull House, was founded by Jane Addams in 1889.[12]

The World's Columbian Exposition became the centerpiece of this cultural expansion. Suggestions for a fair to celebrate the 400th anniversary of Columbus's discovery of the New World were heard by the early 1880s, not long after Philadelphia had hosted a major fair to celebrate the centennial of the Declaration of Independence. By 1882, various people were promoting fairs honoring Columbus in such unlikely places as Mexico City. The first serious mention of a fair to be held in Chicago came from a Chicago dentist, Dr A. W. Harlan, in early 1882. Harlan noted that the city's central location, transportation network, and moderate summer weather would make it an ideal location for a world's fair.

The idea of an 1892 fair continued to attract attention during the 1880s, with Philadelphia, St Louis, Washington, and New York all proposed as potential host cities. Civic leaders in Chicago remained mildly interested as well, but not until 1888 did they begin to take seriously the notion that a major world's fair could actually be held in their city.[13]

In May 1888, the influential Iroquois Club passed a resolution supporting a Chicago fair in 1892, and in July, a meeting of representatives from a large number of social and political clubs echoed that sentiment. The great Paris exposition of 1889 gave promoters pause, since it was generally expected that each major world's fair should surpass its predecessor in size and grandeur.

In 1889, Chicago newspapers took up the cause of a fair and found it a popular issue, and in July, Mayor DeWitt Cregier asked the city council to create a 'citizen's committee' to bring the fair to Chicago. Although the committee eventually grew to include 250 members, most of the work was done by an executive committee chaired by Mayor Cregier and including an array of Chicago's most prominent business leaders. In August, the committee obtained a corporation charter from the state in order to allow it to raise money through the sale of stock.[14]

In order to learn what it was up against in Paris, the committee sent a delegation headed by Edward T. Jeffrey, an executive committee member, and Octave Chanute, an engineer, to visit the exposition there and prepare a report on its major features. Jeffrey and his delegation spent six weeks in Paris, and his report, published as *Paris Universal Exposition, 1889* (1889?), was very influential in determining the nature of the World's Columbian Exposition.[15]

While the Jeffrey report gave the Chicago committee something to build on, the Paris fair had emboldened New York civic leaders to make a serious challenge to host the 1892 fair, and many observers believed that New York, the nation's largest commercial center and port city, was the most appropriate site. The other principal contender for the fair was St Louis, which could also claim the advantage of being a centrally located commercial city with an excellent transportation network. Between the late summer of 1889 and the spring of 1890, representatives of the three cities lobbied and propagandized for the sanction of Congress that would determine the victor in the rivalry. Chicago's publicists pointed to St Louis' near South location, which would raise sectional conflicts, and the relative poverty of its people, which would undermine the city's ability to host a fair. New York tried to brush Chicago off as just a 'windy city,' with no pretense of culture. Charles A. Dana advised his *New York Sun* readers: 'Don't pay any attention to the nonsensical claims of that windy city. Its people could not build a world's fair even if they won it.' In its defense, Chicago pointed to its remarkable recovery from the 1871 fire, its ability to represent the large midwestern region and all of its states, and the fact that having the fair in Chicago would allow European visitors to see much more of the United States. The monthly publicity magazine of the fair proudly stated: 'As it was true of old, that all roads led to Rome, it is equally true that all roads lead to Chicago.'[16]

The US Congress began its consideration of the matter in January 1890, and after lengthy and often raucous hearings, the House of Representatives chose Chicago over New York, St Louis, and Washington on 24 February. During the Senate debate, the well-organized and wealthy Chicago committee announced that it was increasing its financial commitment to the fair to $10 million; this expression of serious intent, as well as Chicago's ability to represent a large number of midwestern states, brought the senators around to Chicago's side in April. President Benjamin Harrison, himself a midwesterner, was probably pleased to sign the enabling act on 28 April. Because of the lateness of the authorization, the act provided that the fair should be held in 1893 rather than 1892.[17]

That there were still some doubts about Chicago's ability to handle such a large undertaking was shown by the decision of Congress to create a national committee to superintend the organization, construction, and management of the exposition. This committee, with representatives from each state and territory, was to work in an undetermined relationship with the Chicago Company, as the local committee came to be known, to put on the fair. It was inevitable that conflict should develop between the two committees. One had the money and the local connections, while the other had been legitimized by Congress, which, it felt, gave it authority over the local committee. In the summer of 1890, the national commission reorganized itself, creating a smaller executive committee that would be headquartered in Chicago and able to act on behalf of the full commission. The national commission selected a director-general for the exposition, George Davis of Chicago, upon the recommendation of the Chicago Company, but insisted on outlining his duties and responsibilities.

While Davis's appointment had involved a degree of co-operation between the two committees, conflict continued into the fall of 1890, until Congress noted that the national commission's expenses between April and September totaled more than $35,000. Subsequent budget cuts forced the committee to settle into much more of an advisory role. Out of this action came a joint meeting of the two committees in which an agreement was reached as to how jurisdiction over the exposition would be shared. While not eliminating all problems, this agreement did allow the Chicago Company to proceed toward the resolution of the next critical problem – just where in Chicago would the fair be held?[18]

In early 1890, while Congress debated the bill selecting the host city for the fair, confident Chicago organizers were trying to find a site for the event. The fairgrounds had to be sufficiently large, available for development, and in a location convenient to visitors. Two alternative sites emerged. The first, advocated by many on the committee, was a site in one of Chicago's public parks. The park system, with several parks laid out to the north, west, and south of the downtown area, had been in place ever since before the fire, and although all of the parks had not yet been improved, they were a matter of considerable civic pride. The second site, advocated by the park board, which did not want any of its improved areas bespoiled by the many buildings and roads of a major fair, was along the lakefront near the downtown area, in approximately the same location as the Chicago Interstate Industrial Exposition. This site seemed to meet all the requirements of the Company: it was large enough, available, and certainly convenient to visitors. The only drawback was that there was not sufficient space for the agricultural and livestock exhibits. These, however, could be placed in Jackson Park, one of the unimproved parks, eight miles south of the downtown district.

But the notion of a dual fair site did not sit well with key members of the Chicago Company. One member, James W. Ellsworth, thought that placing the entire fair in Jackson Park would be the way by which the city could get the park improved according to the design made many years earlier by Frederick Law Olmsted, the noted landscape architect. Ellsworth convinced Olmsted to come to Chicago and consult with the fair organizers. He examined various sites, developed a rough plan for the partial use of Jackson Park, and was named consulting landscape architect to the exposition in August.

In September, the organizing committee selected Daniel H. Burnham and John W. Root as consulting architects. This was a natural choice, as they had been partners in Chicago for fifteen years and were the city's best-known architectural firm. Specializing in commercial building, Burnham and Root were responsible for a number of downtown Chicago's most highly regarded skyscrapers, including the Rookery (1886) and the Monadnock building (1891). In addition, the architects were social friends of many members of the Chicago Company and had been doing preliminary work on prospective sites for nearly a year. As the official architects, Burnham and Root found themselves in the middle of the site dispute. Further problems with the lakefront site, particularly with respect to the rights of the Illinois Central Railroad, whose lines ran straight through the proposed site, turned the Company's thinking again toward Jackson Park. At the request of the Company, Burnham presented a site plan utilizing Jackson Park on 21 November, and on 1 December, the Company approved the plan, and the building of the fair commenced along the lines of that plan. Burnham became chief of construction, while Root was appointed supervising architect.[19]

Burnham's plan, worked out in conjunction with Root, Olmsted, and Olmsted's assistant, Henry S. Codman, proposed that the major exhibition buildings comprise a 'Court of Honor,' grouped around a formal body of water. Another body of water, a lagoon, would be situated in more natural surroundings and have a large island in its center. Other fair buildings would be arranged more informally around the lagoon and in other areas of the large site. Burnham knew that there was more architectural work in this plan than his office could possibly handle, so he decided to bring in a team of architects of his own choosing, rejecting the idea of a competition as too time-consuming and too likely to result in mediocrity.

Burnham's choices were some of the great names in American architecture: Richard Morris Hunt, George B. Post, and the firm of McKim, Mead & White of New York, Peabody & Stearns of Boston, and Van Brunt and Howe of Kansas City. While some questioned Burnham's failure to include any other Chicago architects, it is probable that his motivation was based on a desire to make the fair a national effort, an 'American enterprise according to which the whole nation can be judged.' Still, the Chicago Company was not entirely pleased, and its Committee on Grounds and Buildings requested that Burnham choose some local architects to design major structures outside the Court of Honor. Those selected were Adler & Sullivan, William L. Jenney, Henry Ives Cobb, Solon S. Beman, and Burling & Whitehouse.[20]

With the site selected, a team of architects assembled, and a general layout of the fair approved, the Chicago Company and Daniel Burnham had only to transform 686 acres of Jackson Park into a fully functioning city. It was no mean feat. Twenty-six months remained until the fair's scheduled opening day of 1 May 1893.

Notes

1   Caroline Kirkland, *Atlantic Monthly* (September 1858), quoted in Robert Cromie, *A Short History of Chicago*, San Francisco, 1984, p. 70.
2   Cromie, *Short History*, pp. 7–13.
3   *Ibid.*, pp. 14–25.
4   *Ibid.*, pp. 28–41, 45–49, 61–64; Ruth McKenna, *Chicago: These First Hundred Years*, Chicago, 1933, pp. 10–20; Reid Badger, *The Great American Fair: The World's Columbian Exposition and American Culture*, Chicago, 1979, pp. 31–32.
5   McKenna, *Chicago*, p. 27.
6   McKenna, *Chicago*, pp. 28–29; Badger, *Great American Fair*, p. 32.
7   McKenna, *Chicago*, pp. 29–30; Badger, *Great American Fair*, p. 33; Perry Duis, *Chicago: Creating New Traditions*, Chicago, 1976, pp. 17, 21–28; Ross Miller, 'Chicago's secular apocalypse: the great fire and the emergence of the democratic hero,' in John Zukowsky (ed.), *Chicago Architecture, 1872–1922*, Munich, 1987, pp. 27–38. For a discussion of the new commerical architecture produced by Chicago architects during this period, see William H. Jordy, *American Architects and Their Buildings*, Volume III – Progressive and Academic Ideals at the Turn of the Twentieth Century, New York, 1972, pp. 1–82, and various essays in Zukowsky, *Chicago Architecture*.
8   *The Inter-State Exposition Souvenir*, Chicago, 1873, pp. 3–24, 33–42, 306–9; Bessie L. Pierce, *A History of Chicago*, III, pp. 19, 475.
9   Badger, *Great American Fair*, pp. 34–39.
10 *Ibid.*, p. 36.
11 The Gilded Age is the 1870–1900 period in US history, notable for the great growth of industry and the rise of an elite class of newly rich persons who liked to show off their wealth through extravagant spending, as in gilded home decorations.
12 Badger, *Great American Fair*, pp. 36–39.
13 *Ibid.*, pp. 44–45.
14 *Ibid.*, pp. 46–49; *Chicago Tribune*, 11 June 1933. The *Tribune* reporter, James O'Donnell Bennett, had also covered the World's Columbian Exposition, and recalled

various of the fair's leaders: Thomas B. Bryan was 'the courtliest man who ever received a timid reporter'; Joseph Medill was the city's 'journalistic thunderer'; and Frank
Logan, a friend of the Art Institute, was known for his 'impassioned waistcoats.'

15 Edward Turner Jeffrey, *Paris Universal Exposition, 1889*, n.p., 1889?, pp. 7–10.
16 Badger, *Great American Fair*, pp. 48–49, 51.
17 *Ibid.*, pp. 50–52.
18 *Ibid.*, pp. 52, 59–61.
19 *Ibid.*, pp. 56–59, 64; Wim de Wit, 'Building an illusion: the design of the World's
Columbian Exposition,' in Neil Harris *et al.*, *Grand Illusions: Chicago's World's Fair
of 1893*, Chicago, 1993, p. 53. Additional information on the site controversy may be
found in the Owen F. Aldis Papers in the Century of Progress Collection at the
University of Illinois at Chicago archives. These papers contain correspondence from
E. S. Jennison, a local architect who favored the lakefront site, to Aldis, a member of
the fair board of trustees.
20 De Wit, 'Building an illusion', pp. 53–55, 57.

2   The World's Columbian Exposition

'It was simply a journey to Fairyland.'[1]

The design of the World's Columbian Exposition, including the architecture of its buildings, has occasioned an abundance of commentary since 1893. Visitors thought that the vista of the White City was the experience of a lifetime and contemporary critics generally praised the elegant formality of the Court of Honor, while dissident architects, notably Louis Sullivan, felt that the derivative architecture set the course toward a truly American architecture back by fifty years. More recent commentators, such as Wim de Wit, have looked at the design and architecture not for what it was, but for what it was supposed to represent. Regardless of the point of view one takes, it is clear that the physical appearance of the World's Columbian Exposition was its most remarkable attribute.

Discussion of the design of the fair – what it should look like – had been going on since 1889 and was predicated on two important points. First, it was necessary to create a fair that would do away with the lack of respect that Chicagoans felt they received from the rest of the nation, and indeed, the lack of respect that many Americans felt they sensed on the part of Europeans. In doing this, the design had to show the unity of the United States and the full-fledged development of its civilization. Moreover, there was an undercurrent of feeling that the fair represented the aim of the United States to take a greater role in world affairs through increased commercial trade, through the sustenance of the frontier syndrome by means of overseas expansion, and through a sense of patriotism and adventure. This was reflected in the fact that Chicago's leading businesspeople made such a determined effort to bring the fair to Chicago.

The second point of design consideration was the perceived necessity to outshine the Paris exposition of 1889. This was seen early in the *Chicago Tribune*'s request that its readers send in designs for an Eiffel-like tower to be constructed for the World's Columbian Exposition. In November 1889, the *Tribune* printed many of the sketches that had been submitted. The chief attribute of all of them appeared to be height; it was imperative that the Chicago tower be taller than the 986-foot Eiffel Tower, regardless of its appearance or structural niceties. A wide variety of fantasy structure designs was submitted, including one shaped like a giant egg, but in May 1890, the *Tribune* announced that a 1,500-foot tower designed by two men from Washington D.C., Charles Kinkle and G. R. Pohl, would be built for the fair and would 'put the Eiffel Tower in the shade.' Financial problems, however, prevented this or any other tower from being built, and the signature structure for the fair became the Ferris wheel, 264 feet high and located at the center of the Midway. Even without a tower, the World's Columbian Exposition managed to surpass the Paris exposition in other ways. It covered 686 acres to just 72 for Paris, and its buildings were, on the whole, much larger than those in Paris; the largest Columbian building had four times the square footage as the largest Paris building.[2]

Much of what the Chicago architects and planners learned about Paris came from E. T. Jeffrey's report. This report had a significant impact on the World's Columbian Exposition in a number of ways. Jeffrey noted in detail how the Parisians made ample provision for entertainment and recreation, with theaters and concert halls, foreign 'villages,' such as Streets of Cairo, featuring exotic Egyptian dancers, a Javanese village, and Spanish gypsies, all available at a reasonable cost to visitors.

Jeffrey also praised the effect of electric lighting at night and in conjunction with fountains, the narrow gauge railroad that took visitors along the Seine River, and the multiplicity of intellectual conferences, called congresses, that featured discussion of important themes by leading authorities. He was impressed with the comprehensive and well-organized exhibits, which included 'everything conceivable and inconceivable, useful and ornamental. . . .' In general, he thought that the Paris fair went a long way toward meeting the universal goal to 'strengthen international ties, hasten the dawn of a lasting peace between the great nations of the earth, and promote the prosperity and happiness of mankind.'

Jeffrey's report on Paris was of great importance in the building and staging of the World's Columbian Exposition. And through it, the Chicago Company was able to meet its objective of outdoing the Paris fair. The French commissioner to Chicago admitted as much when he said, 'At Paris, our exposition buildings were such as one would naturally expect to find at Chicago, but at Chicago, you have erected palaces such as no one would expect to see anywhere but at Paris.'[3]

The process of creating a design for the fair that would reflect a unified American culture and surpass the Paris effort began in December 1890, when the eastern architects met in the offices of McKim, Mead & White and decided to adopt a neo-classical architectural style and a common cornice height for the buildings in the Court of Honor, basing their decision on Burnham's desire that the fair reflect a 'unified composition.' Although in their own practices the eastern architects did not all employ the neo-classical style, with its Greek and Roman motifs, they had all attended the Ecole des Beaux-Arts in Paris, then the leading architectural school in the world, and had learned the fundamentals of classical design. Burnham, who did not attend the December meeting, was nevertheless pleased and intrigued. He had not gone to the Ecole des Beaux-Arts, but he was conservative in his architectural thinking, and to him, the formal classical style chosen by the easterners was rather new and exciting, but eminently suitable.

The choice of a classical style for the exposition's buildings was a popular one among contemporary critics, Louis Sullivan's view notwithstanding. Montgomery Schuyler, the leading architectural writer of the time, defended the choice as reasonable in order to assure a certain degree of unity and noted that even with the classical style, there was ample opportunity for diversity. Moreover, such a formal, distinguished styling of the buildings indicated good taste and signified that there was indeed an American civilization that could function on the same esthetic plane as European civilization.[4]

The eastern architects came to Chicago to meet with Burnham and Root and the Chicago architects and to see the site for the first time in January 1891. They constituted themselves as an advisory committee with Richard Morris Hunt as chairman and attended a dinner hosted by the Committee on Buildings and Grounds, at which Burnham predicted that the fair would be the third greatest event in American history, following the Declaration of Independence and the Civil War.

The next day the advisory committee met, and the Chicago architects subscribed to the plan to design the fair along classical lines. Absent from the meeting was John Root, who had become ill the previous night. Root soon developed pneumonia and died just three days later.

Root's death shocked the architects and may well have fundamentally altered the look of the World's Columbian Exposition. Always the more creative of the Burnham & Root partnership, Root had studied the Paris fair thoroughly, come to the conclusion that the Chicago fair should be an 'expression of the heartland,' and envisioned a fair with buildings painted in a variety of colors. After Root's death, Charles McKim persuaded Burnham to use white for all the buildings in the Court of Honor. Another eastern architect, Charles B. Atwood, replaced Root on the advisory board, and the fair became, in the words of one critic, a 'gleaming white advertisement of eastern taste.'[5]

Whether the fair reflected eastern taste or not is debatable, but in February 1891, the architects were primarily concerned with getting their white classical buildings from the drawing boards to the Jackson Park site. Although Burnham, in his account of the fair, saw the site as having seven distinct areas, it is easier to comprehend it as a three-part plan. The Court of Honor, located at the south end of the park, included the formal body of water known as the Basin and the major exhibition halls flanking it: the Manufactures and Liberal Arts building, the Electricity building, the Administration building, the Machinery building, and the Agricultural building.

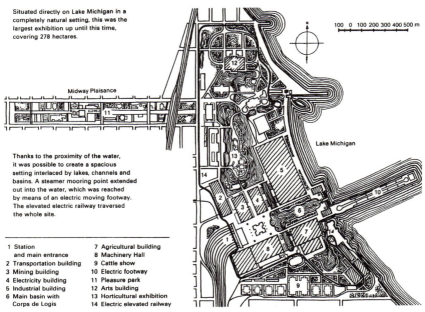

Situated directly on Lake Michigan in a completely natural setting, this was the largest exhibition up until this time, covering 278 hectares.

100 0 100 200 300 400 500 m

Midway Plaisance

Lake Michigan

Thanks to the proximity of the water, it was possible to create a spacious setting interlaced by lakes, channels and basins. A steamer mooring point extended out into the water, which was reached by means of an electric moving footway. The elevated electric railway traversed the whole site.

1 Station
  and main entrance
2 Transportation building
3 Mining building
4 Electricity building
5 Industrial building
6 Main basin with
  Corps de Logis
7 Agricultural building
8 Machinery Hall
9 Cattle show
10 Electric footway
11 Pleasure park
12 Arts building
13 Horticultural exhibition
14 Electric elevated railway

1 Site plan of the World's Columbian Exposition, 1893.

Stretching north and west of the Court of Honor, the second area of the site encompassed the lagoon and Wooded Island, the Fine Arts building, the Transportation building, the Horticultural building, the Fisheries building, the Mines and Mining building, the Women's building, and all the state and foreign nation buildings. This area took in the north end of the park and like Jeffrey had seen at the Paris exposition, featured many of the buildings in a natural, wooded setting.

The third area of the exposition was Midway Plaisance, a mile-long street that ran west from Jackson Park near the Women's building to Washington Park. Along the Midway, as it soon became known, were all the entertainment venues, as well as a number of quasi-anthropological exhibits in the form of native 'villages,' which strove to bridge the gap between entertainment and education.[6]

As chief of construction, Burnham faced the daunting task of supervising the building of the fair in little more than two years. Before construction could begin, however, much work had to be done to improve the site and create the waterways around which the buildings would be placed. Dredging and filling began in February 1891 under the direction of young Henry S. Codman, Olmsted's principal associate at the fair site. Codman was something of a revelation to Burnham and the architects. Only twenty-seven in 1891, Codman had a genuine talent for landscaping in a formal manner; it was said that 'nature spoke through him direct.' His was a monumental task. Over one million square yards of earth were moved to create the Basin, the Lagoon, and the connecting canals, to improve the lakefront beach area, and to build a 1,500-foot pier out into the lake to receive visitors arriving by boat.

Actual construction began on 2 July with groundbreaking for the Mines and Mining building and proceeded rather rapidly because of iron and steel framing techniques, relatively new in construction, and the use of staff, a substance made of plaster, cement, and fiber that was malleable, paintable, and relatively cheap and easy to work with. Applied over wood lath and painted, and formed into ornamental sculpture, staff gave the appearance of a much more permanent and elegant wall surface. As a time-saving device, the decision to paint the buildings in the Court of Honor white was extended to all the other major buildings, except Louis Sullivan's Transportation building, and a powered paint sprayer was devised. Even more time was saved by leaving the interiors of the exhibition buildings unfinished, except for the Administration building, which was used for meetings and fair business rather than the display of exhibits.[7]

Mindful of the Haymarket Riot, Burnham took a cautious approach in hiring workers, rejecting union demands for a closed shop and insisting that security personnel be native-born. Despite his precautions, there were occasional strikes, but safety was a more serious problem; 18 workers were killed and over 700 were injured in work-related accidents on the site in 1891 alone.

While the fair was under construction, Burnham was also generating as much publicity as possible for the event by allowing visitors on the site for an admission fee of twenty-five cents (later raised to fifty cents), despite the fact that they often got in the way of the work. Moses Handy, the official public relations agent for the exposition, published a guide-book in August 1892 for the benefit of people visiting the site during construction. For a cost of ten cents, visitors could use the book to tell which building was which and to get a notion of the layout of the fair. Several thousand people a day came to the site during the construction period, many on the Illinois Central Railroad, which ran special trains every twenty minutes from downtown Chicago to the site for twenty-five cents round trip.

Burnham also insured good publicity for the fair by personally escorting groups of visiting public officials and other dignitaries around the site and by employing Charles Dudley Arnold, a photographer from Buffalo, New York, to make the official photographic record of the fair's construction. Arnold's excellent photographs, printed using a platinum process, give the fair, even under construction, an almost dream-like quality; on a more mundane level, they were used as the basis for many lithographs and engravings of fair scenes that found their way into various forms of promotional material.[8]

Work was interrupted on 21 October 1892 for an elegant dedication ceremony on the site, although the work was barely more than half completed. Held in the largest building, the Manufactures and Liberal Arts building, which had been rushed to virtual completion the month before, the ceremony attracted over 100,000 people. The conductor of the Chicago Orchestra, Theodore Thomas, assembled a symphony orchestra of 500 players and a chorus of 5,500 voices to provide appropriate music, and a host of fair officials and visiting dignitaries, including Vice President Levi P. Morton, gave florid speeches.

In the six months between the dedication and opening day, 1 May 1893, work continued at a frantic pace. A second consecutive harsh winter created delays, as did continuing labor problems, persistent leaky roofs, and accidents. As a consequence, the fair was not quite finished by opening day, and work continued for several more weeks.[9]

Most visitors entered the fairgrounds at the west end of the Court of Honor, if they came by train, or at the east end, if they arrived by boat. Thus, the spectacle of the Court of Honor was the first sight most people saw. It was something they never forgot. Five massive neo-classical buildings, with cornices at a uniform height, painted a dazzling white, and supremely ornamented, surrounded the formal Basin. At the east end of the waterway stood Daniel Chester French's 65-foot tall, gilded *Statue of the Republic*, and at the west end was Frederick William MacMonnies' Columbian Fountain, an allegorical representation of the discovery that the fair was celebrating.

In the Court of Honor, the two most remarkable buildings were Richard Morris Hunt's Administration building and George B. Post's Manufactures and Liberal Arts building. The Administration building, near MacMonnies' statue at the west end of the court, dominated the vista by virtue of its large black and gold dome. For visitors who approached the building, there was an abundance of text and symbolic statuary that ranged from episodes in the life of Columbus to sculpture that indicated America's progress through the years. The Manufactures and Liberal Arts building was noteworthy for its size. At 787 feet wide and 1,687 feet long, it was the largest building in the world at the time of its construction. Its central feature was a 125-foot tall clock tower. It had accommodated over 100,000 for the dedication ceremony, and during the fair, it contained among its 44 acres of exhibits 'pavilions' from many nations displaying the latest in their industrial production.[10]

Moving away from the Court of Honor into the northern part of the park, where the arrangement of buildings was more informal, visitors would probably have paid particular notice to the Transportation building, designed by Louis Sullivan, and to the Fine Arts building, designed by Charles B. Atwood. Sullivan's building stood apart from the other major exhibition buildings because of its 'golden' doorway. The Chicago architect departed from the standard neo-classical style of the fair and created a huge Romanesque entryway, with five concentric semi-circular arches leading visitors into the building. The entrance was painted in bright shades of red, orange, and yellow, and was full of Sullivanesque ornamentation, largely drawn from nature but containing Islamic and Byzantine symbols. But even Sullivan was not oblivious to the fact that the fair was to show the progress of civilization; relief sculpture near the base of the entrance contrasted ancient and modern modes of transportation. Ironically, Sullivan, who popularized the dictum 'form follows function,' did not design a very functional building. Interior space was limited, and some of the most important exhibits had to be relegated to an annex. It might have been worse still had not Burnham persuaded Sullivan to make one large entry instead of two smaller ones.[11]

Charles B. Atwood, who had replaced Root in 1891, designed over sixty buildings for the fair, as well as many ornamental features, but his Fine Arts building is regarded as his most successful work. Burnham thought it was the most beautiful building he had ever seen. Architecturally, it was the most Greek-influenced building among the major structures, but the overall design was very compatible with the buildings of the Court of Honor, and indeed, its location served as a kind of transition point between the formal arrangement of most of the largest exhibition buildings and the smaller state and foreign buildings, situated informally in a previously developed part of the park. Alone among the fair buildings, the Fine Arts building had masonry walls covered by staff; this was necessitated by fire safety concerns for the many valuable works of art and by the fact that fair organizers planned for this building to be used after the fair.[12]

Some thirty-nine states and eighteen foreign nations erected their own pavilions on small lots surrounding the Fine Arts building at the north end of the site. State pavilions were supposed to be representative of some aspect of the state's history or character, but designs had to be submitted to Burnham's office for advance approval. Burnham's essential conservatism showed through when he rejected Montana's plan to build a pavilion in the shape of an artificial mountain, noting that '[it] will be an exceedingly ugly thing.' South Dakota's Sioux tepee met a similar fate; '[it] will present a rather startling effect from an artistic and architectural standpoint.' The South Dakotans were told to design something more in harmony with their neighbors. Although Burnham approved other state designs, the overall effect did not please critic Montgomery Schuyler, who believed that 'picturesque irregularity' succeeded only when a building was considered by itself; such irregularity at the World's Columbian Exposition produced, in his words, a 'higgledy-piggledy' appearance.

Still, Schuyler did see state buildings he liked. The Massachusetts building, a replica of the colonial house of John Hancock, was a very successful effort and made the critic think that each of the former colonies should have been induced to design a colonial-style pavilion. The Swiss

2 Main Concourse. This vista, with its classically designed buildings, painted a dazzling white, gave most visitors their most enduring image of the World's Columbian Exposition.

3 Looking west from the Peristyle. From this point, visitors looked across the Basin to Frederick MacMonnies' Columbian Fountain and the Administration building.

4 Columbian Fountain. Frederick MacMonnies, one of America's leading sculptors, designed this highly allegorical representation of Columbus. Its' night-time illumination made it particularly spectacular.

5 Exhibits in the Manufactures and Liberal Arts building of the World's Columbian Exposition were grouped together by country of origin, with each participating country exhibiting its special crafts and manufactured goods.

6 Manufactures and Liberal Arts building, interior, Austrian section.

7 Walkways along the roof of the Manufactures and Liberal Arts building provided excellent views in every direction.

8 The US Government building, designed by federal government architects and located behind the Manufactures and Liberal Arts Building away from the Main Concourse, was judged by most critics to be a monumental architectural failure.

9 Designed by Chicago architect Henry Ives Cobb, the Fisheries building was one of the more original and distinctive pieces of architecture at the World's Columbian Exposition, 1893.

10 The Agricultural building, designed by the firm of McKim, Mead & White, was located on the man concourse across from the Manufactures and Liberal Arts building. Its interior was described by a contemporary observer as 'a sample room for Mother Nature.'

11 Japan's contribution to the World's Columbian Exposition, the Ho-o-den, was a replica of an eleventh century temple. Frank Lloyd Wright's interest in Japanese design was kindled by this structure.

12 Although there was no Midway attraction called the Arabian Village, this illustration is representative of the Arab section, where there was an Algerian and Tunisian exhibit and a popular feature known as the Streets of Cairo.

13 The Samoan Village, sometimes called the South Sea Islander Village, was a Midway feature located next to the Vienna Café. It was one of the anthropological exhibits that confirmed most visitor's notions of their racial superiority.

chalet-like New Hampshire building, suggesting the mountains of that state, and the festive Spanish-Italian building of Texas were well done, as was Nebraska's colonial building. Some state buildings, like New York's Italian Renaissance villa, were too similar to the original model to be distinguished, while others, like California's Spanish Renaissance building, incorporated just the right amount of neo-classic influence.

On the other hand, Schuyler reserved his severest criticism for the building of the host state, Illinois. The most costly of the state structures, with an ungainly dome of disproportionate size, the Illinois building was, in Schuyler's words, the 'most incongruous and intrusive of all the edifices.' He reserved his most biting scorn for the dome, which 'is not only the ugliest dome on the grounds, but one of the ugliest in the world.' Moreover, it was visible from nearly any point in the park and blocked the view of the Fine Arts building from the canal.[13]

From the beginning, international participation had been important to the organizers of the World's Columbian Exposition, and planning for this had begun in the Department of Foreign Affairs and Ethnology in October 1890. The fair sent representatives to Europe and South America during the summer of 1891 looking for exhibits and inviting foreign governments to construct pavilions. So many accepted that siting the foreign pavilions became something of a problem for Olmsted and Codman. Most nations found themselves near the state pavilions in the north end of the park, but a few were relegated to village style settings on the Midway. As with the states, foreign nations were required to send a preliminary design to Chicago, where Atwood and Codman would approve it and determine a site for it. On the whole, foreign pavilions tended to be more distinctive and traditionally-styled than either the state pavilions or the buildings on the Court of Honor, and most foreign nations attempted in their design to reflect something of their culture. Of the various foreign buildings, Germany's was the most expensive, and its eclectic style impressed visitors as 'one of the most remarkable buildings.' Japan obtained permission to place its building on Wooded Island over the objections of Olmsted, who argued strongly that the island should remain unimproved and be a place of rest for visitors. But Burnham liked Japanese design ('They . . . do the most exquisitely beautiful things.') and overruled Olmsted. The Japanese pavilion, Ho-o-den, was modeled after an eleventh century temple, was a major influence in the architectural development of Frank Lloyd Wright, then a young Chicago architect just beginning his own practice, and was left to the city of Chicago after the fair.[14]

By contrast, the Midway contained no architecture of distinction, with the possible exception of the Ferris wheel, designed by George W. G. Ferris, a Pennsylvania civil engineer. This enormous machine, which was really more of an engineering marvel than a piece of architecture, was 264 feet high and carried 2,160 people when all its thirty-six cars were filled.[15] In addition, the Midway contained native exhibits that were in some cases privately organized, and in others sponsored by foreign governments. There was a purposeful effort to emphasize the cultural aspects of a group of people in order to encourage the study of ethnology, and, as Robert Rydell has pointed out, for visitors to be shown convincing evidence of the racial superiority of the Anglo-Saxon race. If a Midway exhibit was from a 'civilized' country, then 'things' like music, food, or crafts were the focus of attention; if the exhibit was from a 'primitive' country (or colony), then people were the focus. The most primitive groups, like the Javanese and the Dahomeans, were regarded like animals in a petting zoo or small children at a church picnic. The noted writer, Richard Harding Davis, must have reflected the feelings of many visitors when he wrote that the Javanese village was 'so odd and dainty and simple, and the little people so like children masquerading in grown-up people's clothes.'

Despite the attempts at anthropological education, the most exciting and controversial Midway attraction was 'Little Egypt,' the exotic dancer at the Streets of Cairo, who performed the 'dans de ventre' or belly dance. By contemporary standards, or even by the standards of the Century of Progress, Little Egypt's dance was quite tame, but her sensuous motions and broad expanse of bare midriff and diaphonous, semi-transparent skirt were new experiences to the vast majority of spectators. Despite the protestations of the guardians of American moral virtue, like Anthony Comstock, the 'hootchy-kootchy,' as the dance came to be known in American slang, was very popular at the fair and became a staple of amusement parks and state fairs for many years.

Although many villagers fared poorly financially, and foreigners as a rule complained about the way they were treated by fair management, the Midway attractions were very popular, and since they all involved an extra charge, the royalty payments helped finance the exposition. The German Village probably attracted two million visitors, about 1.5 million rode the Ferris wheel, and most of the other villages had about a million admissions.[16]

It was the fact that the only exhibit of black people at the fair was the

Dahomean village on the Midway that upset Frederick Douglass, who saw the village as designed only to reflect blacks as barbarians. He and Ida B. Wells wrote a tract, 'The Reason Why the Colored American is Not in the World's Columbian Exposition,' and while Wells boycotted Colored People's Day (featuring 2,500 watermelons), Douglass used the occasion to speak out against the federal government's failure to stem discrimination and lynching.[17]

The Midway also left a significant legacy in the form of a new kind of urban entertainment devoid of cultural value that sprung up at American cities and resorts. This was the commercialized amusement park, featuring, like the Midway, a melange of rides, sideshow attractions, and other opportunities for visitors to escape the stresses of city life. Coney Island, just outside of New York City, was the prime example. Developed as a beach resort in the early nineteenth century, Coney Island was known for its comfortable hotels and sedate amusements until the 1890s. After the success of the World's Columbian Exposition Midway, however, entrepreneurs began to bring similar attractions to Coney Island, and by 1904, three amusement parks had been constructed, complete with 'hootchy-kootchy' dancers, freak shows, and rides that were even more exciting than the Ferris wheel. The success of Coney Island's parks, as well as one, fittingly named White City, built near Jackson Park in Chicago, spawned amusement parks in most major American cities and traveling carnival shows that provided similar entertainment in small-town and rural America.[18]

Exhibits in the major exhibition halls of the World's Columbian Exposition were cluttered, static, and largely repetitive. In the Manufactures and Liberal Arts building, nations erected their own pavilions, fronted by an ornate façade that had to be approved by the fair management. These were large spaces in a large building; Germany, France, and Great Britain were each allocated over 100,000 square feet. Inside these spaces were exhibits of the best each country had to offer in what was then called 'industrial arts': furniture, jewelry, bronzework, enamels, silver, porcelain, glassware, and decorative ironwork. Similar exhibits were to be found in the other major buildings, and some were disappointed that there were so few operating machines. But many visitors were pleased to see that American technology had caught up to that of Europe; American machine tools, in particular, received much praise but caused a German critic to scoff, 'Everything is done by machine: stamped, pressed, cast, turned, by the dozen, hundred, or thousand, . . . it has no individual character.' Nevertheless, the commercial exhibits were deemed important enough to the business community that twenty-four boxcars full of industrial products exhibited at the fair were sent to Philadelphia, where William P. Wilson, the curator of that city's Commercial Museum, organized them in such a way that visiting businesspeople could learn how to make the best advantage of them, especially in the context of foreign trade. Wilson's task was so immense that his museum did not open until 1899, in collaboration with the National Export Exposition in Philadelphia that year.[19]

Whether the average fairgoer exulted over the machine tool display is problematical. There were a legion of guidebooks published for the exposition, and most did not pay any special attention to the machine tools. One of the most compelling of the guidebooks was *The Time-Saver*, whose sub-title, 'A Book Which Names and Locates 5,000 Things at the World's Fair that Visitors Should Not Fail to See,' spells out the purpose of the book. Put together by a team of 'bright newspaper men,' *The Time-Saver* takes the visitor through the entire fair, building by building and down the Midway, and using a three step rating system, gives every significant exhibit or attraction a '1' (Interesting), '2' (Very Interesting), or '3' (Remarkably Interesting). Thus, visitors with only a limited amount of time could confine themselves to those exhibits awarded a '3' rating. To their credit, the compilers of the book were quite judicious in handing out their ratings, and only a small fraction of the 5,000 items listed were deemed 'remarkably interesting.' These tended to be the more exotic or historically significant exhibits. For example, a Japanese iron eagle, 2 feet high, with 3,000 individually handcrafted feathers, located in the Manufactures and Liberal Arts building, was a '3', as was a 26-foot section of California redwood with a stairway through it. The guns that fired the first and last shots of the Civil War, the original manuscript copy of the Declaration of Independence, and the couch that Union General U.S. Grant sat on at Appamatox were all top-rated historical exhibits. The reporters found the Midway less attractive than many visitors evidently did, awarding a top rating only to the Ferris wheel, and giving a '2' to each of several native villages and Hagenbeck's Zoological Arena.[20]

The Time-Saver did give its top rating to a number of paintings in the Fine Arts exhibit, although it is something of a wonder that the compilers could find anything they may have been looking for. The Fine Arts building contained 9,000 works of art, most by European artists, some by artists from the United States, and few by Canadians, Mexicans, and Japanese painters. Most reviewers thought that the quantity of work overwhelmed what little quality there was; the artworks were hung three or four deep on the walls, as if the ultimate objective was to cover every square foot of wall space.[21]

In a preview article on the fair published in November 1892, *The Dial* magazine noted that the exhibits themselves would not be intellectually stimulating, but that the World's Congress Auxiliary, a separate organization from the Chicago Company, would be holding a series of congresses to which the public would be invited. E. T. Jeffrey, in his report on the Paris exposition of 1889, had discussed similar congresses held in conjunction with that fair, and Charles C. Bonney, who first proposed the idea and then headed the World's Congress Auxiliary, probably borrowed it from Paris. According to *The Dial*, the 'ambitious programme' of the Auxiliary was '[t]o sum up the achievements of the intellect to date, and to indicate the lines of future progress.' The idea attracted a great deal of attention, and was particularly appealing to the Chicago Company, which saw it as another way to dispel the frontier image of the city.

After extensive planning, a very comprehensive program of congresses met at the Art Institute between 15 May and 28 October 1893. Topics ranged from medicine and surgery to Africa, from temperance to literature, but the two most significant were probably the World's Congress of Representative Women, which opened the series of congresses in May, and the World's Parliament of Religions, the largest congress, held over seventeen days in September and followed by an eight-day conference on missionary activity. The women's congress stopped far short of being a public appeal for suffrage, but it did showcase many women from different countries who had made remarkable achievements in science, education, or the arts. The idealistic goal of the world's parliament of religions was to bring people of various religions together to discuss what they had in common and what they had contributed to one another. While most of the participants were American, there was significant representation from India, Japan, and a number of European countries.[22]

The World's Columbian Exposition quietly closed its gates on 31 October, the elaborate closing ceremonies cancelled because of the assassination of Chicago's mayor, Carter H. Harrison, just three days earlier. A total paid attendance of 21,477,212 was recorded, more than twice that of the Centennial Exposition in Philadelphia but less than that of the Paris exposition of 1889. After all the bills were paid, private investors shared a small surplus, a noteworthy achievement during a national depression.[23]

As the fair drew to a close, some Chicagoans mused about the future of the fair buildings, wondering if it might be nice to keep the Court of Honor intact as 'a sort of Venice of pleasure and beauty,' although it was realized that a great deal of expense would be necessary to make the buildings into permanent structures. On 1 January 1894, the grounds were turned over to the park board, and the public was given free access to the site. A wave of vandalism immediately ensued, and on 8 January a fire, probably set deliberately, destroyed the Casino, Peristyle, and Music Hall, and damaged the Manufactures and Liberal Arts building. Further damage occurred as the park became a refuge for vagrants and others suffering in the national depression, and a much larger fire in early July destroyed the rest of the Court of Honor and several other major buildings.

Following the July fire, the remaining buildings on the site, except for the Fine Arts building, were demolished or moved to other locations. The salvageable steel went to the Illinois Steel Company and various plants in Pittsburgh, and 500,000 square feet of glass was sold to florists and cornice men. The Wisconsin building was moved to Kansas City and reconstructed as a men's club, and the Rhode Island building found a new site in the south side of Chicago. A statue of Benjamin Franklin was purchased by the University of Pennsylvania, and a statue of a cowboy and an Indian on horseback went to the city of Denver. Fair company president Harlow N. Higinbotham secured four concrete lions that had reposed near the south lagoon and took them to his farm in suburban Elgin. As for the Fine Arts building, retailer Marshall Field provided the greater part of the $1.5 million that transformed the building into the Field Columbian Museum, which featured natural history exhibits, many of which had been seen at the fair itself. Except for the museum, virtually all of the fair's structures were gone from Jackson Park by the spring of 1896.[24]

Contemporary and immediate post-fair reviews of the World's Columbian Exposition were generally quite favorable. Montgomery Schuyler noted that the real success of the fair was the architectural unity of the Court of Honor, made possible by decreeing the use of classical forms and a uniform cornice line. He also cited the landscape plan as another key to the fair's success, pointing out the skill necessary to effect smooth transitions from the formal Basin to the irregular lagoon and from the setting of the formal classical buildings to the more picturesque structures, such as the Fisheries and Transportation buildings. But, he reminded his readers, these were illusory buildings, or 'holiday' buildings; noting that

Burnham himself had said that the fair is 'an illusion that has here been provided for our delight.'[25]

Edmund Mitchell, writing in *Engineering Magazine*, asserted that world's fairs were more than 'carnivals of pleasure.' He felt that the industrial exhibits were a marvelous learning opportunity for visitors from other countries, citing how the Swiss watch industry had learned about the advantages of US machine-made watches at Philadelphia in 1876, had adopted the American process, and had come to Chicago with their own machine-made watches that were the equal of American watches in quality. It is clear, wrote Mitchell, that 'a well-arranged international exposition becomes virtually a clearing-house of ideas for the whole civilized world.'[26]

It was the notion of the fair as a self-contained city that was particularly attractive to John Coleman Adams, a writer for *New England Magazine*. He praised the systematic planning that one noticed immediately upon entering the fairgrounds – in the streets, building arrangement, and landscaping. He was impressed with the cleanliness of the site, the courtesy of the security staff, and the public drinking fountains and restrooms; all of these features might be found in an 'ideal' city, and all were accessible to the average citizen once he or she had paid the fifty cents to enter the fairgrounds.[27]

While most foreign visitors thought that the World's Columbian Exposition was the greatest fair ever, there were dissenting voices from Britain. Put off, perhaps, by the late completion of the fair, or the highly protective tariff the US Congress had passed in 1890, the *Saturday Review* of London said that the exposition was a good 'local' show, with fine buildings in a conventional classical architecture style and costs that were willingly borne by the local sponsors. But it was a show that offered no reason for anyone outside of Chicago to attend. The exhibits could be seen in any shop window, the meetings of the World's Congress Auxiliary were largely ignored, and the skimpy official guidebook was no help. The review smugly concluded that the best time to go was at night, when the exhibits were closed, and the buildings looked better under the array of electric lights.[28]

A few years after the fair, Joseph M. Rogers, a writer for *Forum*, reflected that the World's Columbian Exposition profited from its site, which 'permitted not only a harmonious distribution of the enormous buildings, but a display of landscape gardening on a scale never before attempted . . . to [which] was added what at the time was a new feature – the great use of electricity.' Another *Forum* writer praised the unity to the fair brought by the use of white on nearly all the major buildings, a much better idea than the 'dangerous and unfortunate' use of color on the buildings at Buffalo's Pan-American Exposition in 1901.[29]

Planning and unity stand as the two key words in remembering the World's Columbian Exposition. Although Louis Sullivan's commentary about the deleterious effects of the classical architecture dominated critical thinking about the fair's impact for many years, contemporary scholars discount the effect the fair's classicism had on the development of an 'American' architecture and point instead to the impetus the fair gave to the city planning movement of the early twentieth century. And more recently, historians like James Gilbert have seen in the fair a deliberate attempt to create a certain 'unified' American culture by using the illusory architecture, the meetings of the World's Congress Auxiliary, and even the photographs of C. D. Arnold to build a consensus of what America should be. While the popularity of the Midway's cruder attractions and the obvious contrasts between the fair and the rest of the city prevented the total achievement of that goal, the fair was the event of a lifetime for many visitors, a model for many subsequent fairs, and a looming presence with which the organizers of the Century of Progress Exposition had to contend some forty years later.[30]

Notes

1 'Literary tributes to the world's fair,' *The Dial*, XV, 1 October 1893, p. 177.

2 Wim de Wit, 'Building an illusion: the design of the World's Columbian Exposition,' in Neil Harris *et al., Grand Illusions: Chicago's World's Fair of 1893*, Chicago, 1993, pp. 45–9.

3 De Wit, 'Building an illusion,' p. 49; James P. Holland, 'Chicago and the world's fair,' *Chautauquan*, XVII, May 1893, pp. 136–39; Edward Turner Jeffrey, *Paris Universal Exposition, 1889*, n.p., 1889?, pp. 14–21.

4 Thomas S. Hines, *Burnham of Chicago: Architect and Planner*, New York, 1974, p. 97; Charles Moore, *Daniel H. Burnham: Architect, Planner of Cities*, Boston, 1921, I, pp. 31–42; de Wit, 'Building an illusion,' pp. 58–61, 66; Jeffrey, *Paris Universal Exposition*, pp. 11–13.

5 David Lowe, *Lost Chicago*, Boston, 1975, pp. 150–52; Robert Knutson, 'The White City: the World's Columbian Exposition of 1893,' unpublished Ph.D. dissertation, Columbia University, 1956, p. 31; Reid Badger, *The Great American Fair: The World's Columbian Exposition and American Culture*, Chicago, 1979, pp. 67–68. According to Charles Moore, McKim came to replace Root in Burnham's life as an artistic and intellectual colleague. McKim, known for his 'rodent-like determination,' made Burnham's romantic ideas practical and became the controlling architectural force of the World's Columbian Exposition. See Moore, *Daniel H. Burnham*, pp. 66–67.

6 De Wit, 'Building an illusion,' p. 74.

7   Robert Muccigrosso, *Celebrating the New World: Chicago's Columbian Exposition of 1893*, Chicago, 1993, p. 74; Badger, *Great American Fair*, pp. 69–71; Moore, *Daniel H. Burnham*, p. 46.

8   Robert V. Sharp (ed.), *Constructing the Fair: Platinum Photographs by C. D. Arnold of the World's Columbian Exposition*, Chicago, 1993, p. 27; Muccigrosso, *Celebrating*, p. 73.

9   Sharp, *Constructing the Fair*, p. 15; Muccigrosso, *Celebrating*, pp. 74–77; Knutson, 'White City,' p. 32.

10   Knutson, 'White City,' pp. 149ff.; de Wit, 'Building an illusion,' pp. 49, 81–85, 88.

11   Hines, *Burnham*, pp. 98–101; de Wit, 'Building an illusion,' p. 92; Muccigrosso, *Celebrating*, pp. 69–70.

12   Badger, *Great American Fair*, p. 104; de Wit, 'Building an illusion,' p. 78; Moore, *Daniel H. Burnham*, pp. 48–49.

13   Hines, *Burnham*, pp. 96–97; Montgomery Schuyler, 'State buildings at the world's fair,' *Architectural Record*, III, July–September, 1893, pp. 58–63, 69–71.

14   Hines, *Burnham*, pp. 108–9; Price Collier, 'The foreign buildings,' *Cosmopolitan*, XV, September 1893, pp. 540–41; Eric Sandweiss, 'Around the world in a day,' *Illinois Historical Journal*, LXXXIV, Spring 1991, pp. 2–10.

15   The Ferris wheel was devised by and named for George Washington Gale Ferris, Jr., a civil engineer and businessman. He contracted with fair officials in late November 1892 to build the attraction on the Midway Plaisance, and it opened on 21 June 1893, about seven weeks after the fair opened. A total of 1,453,611 ride tickets were sold at fifty cents each. After the fair, the Ferris wheel operated in a park on Chicago's north side for several years before making a final appearance at the Louisiana Purchase Exposition in St Louis in 1904. It was dismantled and sold for scrap in 1906. See Norman D. Anderson, *Ferris Wheels: An Illustrated History*, Bowling Green, Ohio, 1992, pp. 42–85.

16   Muccigrosso, *Celebrating*, pp. 165–68; Sandweiss, 'Around the world,' pp. 10–12; Robert Rydell, *All the World's a Fair*, Chicago, 1984, pp. 60–68; Richard Harding Davis, 'The last days of the fair,' *Harper's Weekly*, XXXVII, 21 October 1893, p. 1002. Many of the 'ethnological exhibits' are pictured in *The Detroit Free Press Portfolio of the Midway Types*, Chicago, 1893.

   C. D. Arnold's photographs and concessionaires' records indicate that the Midway was considerably more popular with visitors than the White City. See James Gilbert, *Perfect Cities: Chicago's Utopias of 1893*, Chicago, 1991, p. 122.

17   Donald L. Miller, 'The White City,' *American Heritage*, XLIV, July–August 1993, p. 85; Rydell, *All the World's a Fair*, pp. 52–53; Muccigrosso, *Celebrating*, pp. 145–47.

18   John Kasson, *Amusing the Millions: Coney Island at the Turn of the Century*, New York, 1978, pp. 26–34.

19   Robert Rydell, 'The culture of imperial abundance,' in Simon J. Bronner (ed.), *Consuming Visions: Accumulation and Display of Goods in America, 1880–1920*, New York, 1989, pp. 210-15; George Frederick Kunz, 'Notes on industrial art in the Manufactures Building,' *Cosmopolitan*, XV, September 1893, pp. 547–59; Joseph M. Rogers, 'Lessons from international exhibitions,' *Forum*, XXXII, November 1901, pp. 508–9.

20   W. Hamilton, *The Time-Saver*, Chicago, 1893, *passim*.

21   Hamilton, *Time-Saver*, pp. 45–57; Muccigrosso, *Celebrating*, pp. 102–7.

22 Clay Lancaster, *The Incredible World's Parliament of Religions*, Fontwell, Sussex, 1987; 'The higher aspects of the Columbian Exposition,' *The Dial*, XIII, 1 November 1892, pp. 263–65; Maurice Neufeld, 'The White City: the beginnings of a planned civilization in America,' *Journal of the Illinois State Historical Society*, XXVII, April 1934, pp. 71–93; Badger, *Great American Fair*, pp. 77–78.

23 Badger, *Great American Fair*, pp. 109, 131. Despite the somber mood brought on by the mayor's death, the Midway on the last day of the fair was marked by 'some hours of unrestrained revelry [that] gave vent to . . . semi-restrained exotic and native depravity.' Charles Dudley Warner, 'The last day of the fair,' *Harper's Weekly*, XXXVII, 11 November 1893, p. 1074.

    Although investors did share in a small surplus after the fair closed, they recovered only a small fraction of their original investment. Century of Progress officials studied the finances of this and other earlier fairs very carefully in their effort to make their fair a sound business proposition.

24 Knutson, 'White City,' p. 270; 'Fate of the Chicago world's fair buildings,' *Scientific American*, LXXV, 3 October 1896, p. 267; Warner, 'The last day of the fair,' pp. 1074–75.

25 Montgomery Schuyler, 'Last words about the world's fair,' *Architectural Record*, III, January–March 1894, pp. 292–99.

26 Edmund Mitchell, 'International effects of the fair,' *Engineering Magazine*, VI, January 1894, p. 471.

27 John Coleman Adams, 'What a great city might be – a lesson from the White City,' *New England Magazine*, n.s., XIV, March 1896, pp. 3–13.

28 Mitchell, 'International effects,' pp. 468–70; 'The Chicago exhibition,' *Saturday Review* (London), LXXVI, 11 November 1893, pp. 538–39.

29 Rogers, 'Lessons,' pp. 504–5; William O. Partridge, 'The educational value of world's fairs,' *Forum*, XXXIII, March 1902, pp. 121–24.

30 Gilbert, *Perfect Cities*, pp. 126–27; Burnham was certain that he knew what the fair signified: 'The intellectual reflex of the Exposition will be shown in a demand for better architecture, and designers will be obliged to abandon their incoherent originalities and study the ancient masters of building.' See Russell Lynes, *The Lively Audience*, New York, 1985, p. 56.

3   From one fair to another

The streets of Cairo, where Little Egypt thrilled visitors to the World's Columbian Exposition with her exotic dancing, will come into glamorous existence again.[1]

The connection between the World's Columbian Exposition and the Century of Progress Exposition is somewhat tenuous, despite the fact that the two fairs took place in the same city just forty years apart. It certainly was not seen in a continuation of historical or even reminiscent writing about the Columbian Exposition. While an abundance of published material about that fair had appeared in the years immediately following the event, including numerous multi-volume official reports, replete with statistics, lists of awards, speeches, and detailed descriptions of buildings, little appeared after 1900.

By the 1920s, the great era of fairs in America had passed, and along with it, direct reference to the World's Columbian Exposition. In that decade of blossoming modernism, the fair began to seem old-fashioned, even anachronistic, and Louis Sullivan's scornful analysis of the architecture, published in 1924, found a sympathetic audience. Sullivan's diatribe was restated in somewhat more genteel language by social and architectural critics like Henry Russell Hitchcock, who characterized the fair as the 'white plague,' and Lewis Mumford, who asserted that the fair had been a grand façade masking much more serious social problems. Planners of the Century of Progress studied the World's Columbian Exposition in considerable detail and doubtless learned much from it, but more often than not, the decisions they made were designed to create a fair that was in sharp contrast to the earlier exposition.[2]

The legacy of the World's Columbian Exposition that lived on into the twentieth century is seen in more indirect ways – the city planning movement and the Burnham Plan of 1909, the continuing attention paid to the old Fine Arts building, and the continuing development of Chicago as a commercial and cultural city. In each of them, there was some homage paid to the World's Columbian Exposition, and from each, the Century of Progress felt some impact.

One of the legacies of the World's Columbian Exposition was that the unity of its physical organization gave people confidence that the lessons of the fair could be used to reform urban life – that cities could be made subject to planning just as the fair had been. The first person to see merit in a city plan for Chicago was a graphic artist named James F. Gookens, who had studied in Munich and drawn Civil War sketches for a number of leading magazines. Gookens moved to Chicago in the late 1860s, was active in art circles, and after the fire, saw a need to do something about the urban chaos brought on by the rapid and uncontrolled rebuilding of the city. Inspired by the World's Columbian Exposition and talk about rebuilding the city like the fair, he drew up a city plan between 1893 and 1903, but he died before the city council could act on it.

Daniel Burnham probably knew Gookens and may well have been aware of his city plan, but evidence suggests that Burnham was influenced more by his service on the Washington D.C. Park Commission, to which he was appointed in 1901. As part of this commission, Burnham worked with others to modernize the original Pierre L'Enfant plan of 1791, and he toured Paris and Versailles as part of his service in Washington. Burnham's work in Washington was done in 1902, and he went on to direct planning efforts in Cleveland (1903), San Francisco (1905), and two Philippine cities, Manila and Baguio (1905).

In 1906, Burnham obtained support from Chicago's Merchants Club, an association of private businessmen which merged with the Commercial Club in 1907. This enabled him to begin work on a plan for Chicago in collaboration with a young associate, Edward H. Bennett, who would later become one of the architects of the Century of Progress. Burnham and Bennett worked for three years on the plan, which was approved by the city council in 1910. Responsibility for implementation was given to the Chicago Plan Commission, created in 1908, and headed by Charles B. Norton and Charles H. Wacker.

The *Plan of Chicago, 1909*, the name under which it was published, is notable for its comprehensive nature, encompassing the entire metropolitan Chicago area. Burnham and Bennett attempted to identify specific problems and devise practical solutions for them, rather than drawing up plans for an entirely new fantasy city. The plan recognized the commercial importance of Chicago by emphasizing transportation in, out, and around the city, and it also recognized the need of working-class people for rest and relaxation and the importance of a city being able to maintain a certain dignity; hence, provisions were made for parkland and public buildings, artfully arranged. The plan guided Chicago's development for fifty years after its adoption. Cost factors and changing circumstances meant that some elements were never implemented, but many features that impinged on the Century of Progress were completed, and the entire document gave life to Burnham's words: 'Make no little plans; they have no magic to stir men's blood. . . . Make big plans; aim high in hope and work'[3]

In its specifics, the Plan of Chicago involved six major elements. First, the plan called for the development of the lakefront opposite the downtown area (called the 'Loop' after the completion of a downtown elevated railroad in 1897), including a yacht harbor, the formal landscaping of Grant Park, the construction of Northerly Island, and the building of a pier or piers out into the lake. Second, there was to be a co-ordinated highway system out to the suburbs, centered on a highway leading directly west out of the Loop. Third, the railroads and their terminals were to be centralized. Fourth, the plan envisioned extensive additions to the park system, including a series of forest preserves in and around the suburbs. Fifth, the street plan within the city was to be systematized, with particular attention paid to widening and straightening Michigan Avenue, and sixth, the Loop was to be redefined as the cultural center of the city, with a variety of new attractions to be built in and near the downtown area.[4]

The Plan of Chicago encountered major financial and legal obstacles that prevented its immediate (and even long-term) implementation in many respects. Some recommendations required new legislation, some might even have required changes in the Illinois constitution, and some laws would have needed to be changed to control more closely what businesses and real estate interests could do with their property. Moreover, Chicago was limited by state regulation in the amount of money it could allocate to public works. That the city was unable to increase its bonded indebtedness in order to raise funds for public works without a constitutional amendment was a major handicap in carrying out the Burnham Plan and probably had some role in slowing the economic growth of the city. Nevertheless, much was done over the years. The lakefront was improved, forest preserves were set aside, Michigan Avenue was straightened and widened, and the Eisenhower Expressway heads straight west to the suburbs from the Loop.[5]

The years between the Plan of Chicago and the Century of Progress witnessed a major commercial building boom in Chicago, with much of the architectural work done by Burnham's firm after his death in 1912. Until at least 1922, the classicism Burnham had favored continued to dominate in the tall office buildings that were constructed, giving at least some credence to Sullivan's commentary about the influence of the fair's architecture. Among the significant buildings built during this period were the Rand-McNally building (1911–12), by Holabird & Roche, in a restrained Gothic style, the Wrigley building (1919–21), by Graham, Anderson, Probst & White, in an eclectic neo-classical style, and the Tribune Tower (1923–25), also by Holabird & Roche, whose Gothic design won an international competition.

Architectural modernism began to appear in Chicago in the mid-1920s with the Lincoln Tower (1927–28), by Herbert Riddle, the Palmolive (now Playboy) building (1928–29) and the *Daily News* building (1928–29), both by Holabird & Root. These structures were notable for their exterior smoothness, attention to geometry, and setbacks. The grandest Chicago building of the 1920s, the Civic Opera Building (1928–29), by Graham, Anderson, Probst & White, likewise contained these features and dominated Wacker Drive on the northwest side of the Loop. All of these buildings, and others besides, marked a tremendous increase in the amount of office space available in downtown Chicago during the 1920s; over three million square feet of rentable space was added in 1927 alone. Of course, the stock market crash of October 1929 and the ensuing depression ended the building boom in the Loop. The last major office tower, the Field building (1931–34), by Graham, Anderson, Probst & White, described as a 'Sullivanesque skyscraper stripped down to essentials,' was the only office building under construction in the entire country at the time it was finished.[6]

The Plan of Chicago's consideration of public buildings, cultural venues, and recreational space represent one of its most valuable contributions, and one that was quite fully implemented prior to the Century of Progress, and a number of the structures that were built played a role in the staging of that exposition. The first civic building following the publication (although not the approval) of the Plan of Chicago was the monumental City Hall and County Building (1909–11), designed by Holabird & Roche and covering an entire city block. This was followed by a new museum of natural history to replace the Field Columbian Museum in Jackson Park. In his will, Marshall Field provided $4 million for such a museum if it could be built within six years of his death. Field died in 1906, and arrangements were quickly made for a museum, designed by Daniel Burnham, to be erected in Grant Park, near the Loop and in keeping with the Plan of Chicago. But Burnham's death in 1912 and a wave of public opposition, centered around a court decision prohibiting construction in Grant Park, delayed the start of construction until 1915. In 1918, the War Department took over the still unfinished museum for use as a hospital for a period of several months, the installation of fixtures took another year, and the Field Museum of Natural History finally opened to the public in June 1920.

After the completion of the museum, a citywide design competition was held for a large stadium that could host athletic events and various civic pageants. The competition rules stipulated that the design had to be compatible with the classical style of the Field Museum, located just to the north of the stadium site, and Holabird & Roche's Greek Revival design prevailed. The architects unified the two structures by repeating decorative elements, using a common axis, and leaving the north end of the stadium open, so spectators could see the museum (although in 1934–35, a park headquarters building was erected in between the stadium and museum, ruining the view).

Just across the street from the Field Museum, the Shedd Aquarium opened in the fall of 1929. The result of a bequest of John G. Shedd, the building was classically styled by Graham, Anderson, Probst & White but featured a highly functional floor plan. Nearby, at the north end of newly built Northerly Island, also called for in the Plan of Chicago, the Max Adler Planetarium was opened in 1930. The work of Chicago architect Ernest Grunsfeld, Jr., the planetarium's design stressed 'dignity and simplicity' and won an American Institute of Architects gold medal in 1930. The cultural center around Grant Park was completed with the construction in 1931 of an orchestra shell for outdoor concerts.[7]

By 1931, construction was well underway at the Century of Progress site, located just south of the museum, aquarium, and planetarium, and east of the stadium. Because of the implementation of Burnham's plan of Chicago, Century of Progress management could tie their fair into this cultural setting, and did so, actually including the planetarium in the fairgrounds, and using the stadium for many exposition-related sporting events and musical pageants.

The final jewel in the cultural tiara of Chicago during the 1920s was the renovation of the old Field Columbian Museum in Jackson Park. After the completion of the new Grant Park museum of natural history in 1920, the old building, still clad in 1893 staff, now vacant and unmaintained, began to deteriorate rapidly. In 1921, George Maher, a Chicago architect and protégé of Frank Lloyd Wright, argued for saving the building and restoring it as a branch of the Art Institute, or using it for some other worthy social or educational purpose. He recommended that the exterior be stripped of staff, redone in waterproof Portland cement plaster, with all the architectural detail and ornament replicated as it had been at the World's Columbian Exposition. Maher estimated that this could be done for $1.64 million, as opposed to the $10 million it would cost to replace the building from the ground up.

Little happened for several years, and the building became a Jackson Park derelict, but in 1926, Julius Rosenwald, the wealthy president of Sears, Roebuck and Company, who had traveled to Europe and been very impressed with the Deutsches Museum, a technology museum in Munich, provided a gift of $3 million to establish an American technology museum. That year, the Museum of Science and Industry received an Illinois state charter, and an additional $4.5 million from Rosenwald allowed the Field Columbian Museum to be completely refurbished and turned into the Rosenwald Museum of Science and Industry. Work began in 1929, and the project was completed in early 1933, not long before the Century of Progress opened. Because that exposition emphasized progress in science and technology, many of its exhibits went to the Museum of Science and Industry after the fair closed in 1934 and helped form the basis of the first generation of museum exhibits.[8]

Just as planning for the World's Columbian Exposition had begun in the wake of a period of civic disorder and violence that had helped spur local leaders to initiate a movement to elevate the cultural ambience of Chicago, so too did planning for the Century of Progress get underway during years of considerable civic unrest. While the decade of the 1920s meant good business and exciting work for Chicago's architects and building contractors, it meant much the same for Chicago's criminal underworld, striving to take advantage of the illicit but highly profitable opportunities offered by the national experiment in the prohibition of the manufacture, distribution, or sale of alcoholic beverages. Organized crime in Chicago and the suburb of Cicero, headed by Al Capone, ushered in a decade of highly public violence, featured by the execution-style murders of many rival mobsters. Chicago's political leaders, notably Mayor William 'Big Bill' Thompson, were often elected with the financial support of organized

crime and were thus compromised in their efforts to restore law and order
to the city's streets. All of this created for Chicago an unsavory reputation and was certainly a factor in the minds of those who were at this
time planning Chicago's second world's fair, the Century of Progress
Exposition.[9]

Notes

1 Century of Progress publicity, quoted in the *New York Times*, 15 February 1933.
2 Neil Harris, 'Memory and the White City,' in Neil Harris *et al.*, *Grand Illusions: Chicago's World's Fair of 1893*, Chicago, 1993, pp. 11–23.
3 Harold M. Mayer and Richard C. Wade, *Chicago: Growth of a Metropolis*, Chicago, 1969, pp. 274–80; Carl W. Condit, *Chicago, 1910–1929*, Chicago, 1973, pp. 59–64.
4 Art Institute of Chicago, *The Plan of Chicago: 1909–1979*, Chicago, 1979, *passim*; Mayer and Wade, *Chicago*, pp. 276–80.
5 'The Chicago plan after fifteen years,' *Western Architect*, XXXV, January 1926, p. 2; Condit, *Chicago*, p. 81.
6 Condit, *Chicago*, pp. 94–135.
7 *Ibid.*, pp. 149–50; 178–205.
8 George W. Maher, 'The restoration of the Fine Arts Building of the world's fair,' *Architectural Forum*, XXXV, June 1921, pp. 35–37; Mayer and Wade, *Chicago*, pp. 200–9.
9 Emmett Dedmon, *Fabulous Chicago*, New York, 1953, pp. 285–300. For additional information dealing with crime in Chicago, the following books are useful: Herbert Asbury, *Gem of the Prairie*, New York, 1940 (reprint edn, Dekalb, Ill., 1986); Lloyd Lewis and Henry Justin Smith, *Chicago: The History of Its Reputation*, New York, 1929; Lloyd Wendt and Herman Kogan, *Lords of the Levee: The Story of Bathhouse John and Hinky Dink*, Indianapolis, 1943, and *Big Bill of Chicago*, Indianapolis, 1953; John Kobler, *Capone: The Life and World of Al Capone*, New York, 1971; John Landesco, *Organized Crime in Chicago*, Chicago, 1968; and Walter C. Reckless, *Vice in Chicago*, Chicago, 1933.

4

Planning Chicago's second world's fair

[Removing squatters from shanties on the fair site] was often heartbreaking, but we had to remember that what we were being paid to do was build a fair, not look after every unfortunate.[1]

In a letter dated 17 August 1923, Chicago minister and social worker Myron E. Adams suggested to Mayor William E. Dever that some kind of exhibition should be held in 1937 to celebrate the centennial of Chicago's incorporation as a city. Such a celebration, which could, Adams wrote, be held even earlier than 1937, would bring about the final realization of Daniel H. Burnham's City Beautiful plan. Adams urged Dever to move ahead with the planning for such an event, involving the public sector to carry out needed civic improvements and the development of a lakefront fair site. He thought Grant Park, adjacent to the central business area of the city, should contain a replica of Chicago as it was in 1837, and noted the availability of the nearby Art Institute, Field Museum of Natural History, and other venues for activities.[2]

During 1924 and 1925, another Chicago businessman, W. E. Clow, a plumbing supplies manufacturer, also urged the holding of a fair for the centennial of Chicago, but his suggestions were rejected by the Commercial Club of Chicago as too risky. Adams's and Clow's suggestions continued to be discussed informally among civic leaders, however. On 1 December 1925, the Chicago Planning Commission and the Chicago Historical Society jointly endorsed the idea and requested the city council to consider it. The council added its endorsement on 8 March 1926, and authorized Mayor Dever to appoint a 150-member organizing committee. Aware of the difficulty that large committees have in accomplishing their goals, the mayor limited the committee to 100, chaired by Edward N. Hurley, and including Rufus Dawes, Charles S. Peterson, and Myron E. Adams.[3]

The organizing committee met frequently between April 1926 and August 1927. In May 1926, the decision was made to celebrate the centennial of Chicago's founding in 1833 with an international exposition. 'Chicago is ripe for a world's fair,' said commission member Alexander H. Revell.[4] In June, Daniel H. Burnham, Jr., son of the architect who had directed the building of the World's Columbian Exposition of 1893 and also a commission member, wrote in the *Chicago Daily News* about the many civic improvements that should accompany the 1933 celebration. Articles such as this began the process of planting the idea of a major centennial celebration in the public mind.[5]

In 1927, however, opposition from financial circles in the city began to mount, and new mayor William 'Big Bill' Thompson, responsive, perhaps, to those who had helped him in his recent election victory, announced in August that the plan was dead. The public outcry to this announcement surprised even the ever-confident mayor, and he asked the city treasurer, Charles S. Peterson, to determine if the people of Chicago truly wanted a centennial fair. By December, Peterson was satisfied that the people did want a fair, and at a meeting on the thirteenth, an organizing committee was created to plan what was referred to as Chicago's 'second world's fair' in 1933. A week later, Rufus C. Dawes, a Chicago construction company executive and the brother of Vice-President Charles Gates Dawes, accepted the presidency of the committee.[6]

From this point, the organizing committee moved very quickly. On 5 January 1928, it was granted a state charter to operate under the awkward but descriptive name of 'Chicago Second World's Fair Centennial Celebration,' and four days later, the Board of Trustees of the committee held its first meeting. Consisting of Dawes as president, Peterson as vice-president, Daniel H. Burnham, Jr., as secretary, and George Woodruff, a prominent banker, as treasurer, this body was the central nervous system of the fair organization for the next six years. In a flurry of activity during the next month, the board adopted a set of by-laws, established working committees for a wide array of fair-related activities, and began the process of financing the fair through the initiation of a drive to sell $5.00 shares, for which the purchaser would receive ten admission tickets to the fair. Although the campaign began slowly, a total of 118,773 shares were sold over the next few years, generating, with interest, $637,754 for the board. More importantly, the campaign served to build public interest in the centennial celebration by giving the ordinary citizen a stake in what was happening.[7]

Generating public interest through the news value of the fair was important because the board of trustees had decided not to utilize any of their limited funds on paid advertising, a technique that had worked well for the World's Columbian Exposition and San Francisco's Panama-Pacific Exposition in 1915. A committee on public information, headed by Homer J. Buckley, was created in April 1928 that kept newspapers and magazines well supplied with exposition information through press releases and news features. Reporters and editors were coddled whenever possible. At a large dinner given in honor of Charles G. Dawes shortly before he went to London as US ambassador to Britain, the board expanded the list of invited press people, noting that 'all newspapermen here enjoy being given Palmer House publicity stunt assignments because they know that Bert Fuller, the house publicity man . . . will see that they are taken to one of the dining rooms and fed. This does not mean that newspapermen as a class are spongers. But they do appreciate being given consideration and being treated like regular people.' On 1 April 1931, the committee on public information began publication of a weekly newsletter named *Progress*, which continued to appear until the fair opened, when it became known as *World's Fair Weekly*, and was oriented more toward informing visitors about the fair. In addition, the Chicago newspapers became important boosters of the Century of Progress, running daily news and feature articles about the people and events connected with the fair. The *Chicago Tribune* even had a daily question and answer column, responding to a wide array of questions that ranged from the obvious to the bizarre: 'Q: Is there an orchestra composed of veterans of the world war, who have lost one or both legs, now playing at the fair? A: No.'[8]

Although Burnham worried about the prospect of a national Washington bicentennial exposition in 1932 – 'it would be very inexpedient for us to hold a big exhibition in 1933 if a national exposition is to be held in Washington or some other place in 1932'[9] – the board continued to move ahead rapidly. In February, an Architectural Commission was created, and as had been the case with the World's Columbian Exposition, a number of the country's leading architects were invited to join. By early 1928, Dawes was meeting informally with members of the National Research Council, an umbrella organization of scientists formed in 1916 to advise the government during World War I; these meetings would help the board focus on scientific progress over the past hundred years as the general theme of the fair.[10]

With the Architectural Commission assuming the responsibility for building design and site planning, and the Science Advisory Committee of the National Research Council poised to develop the central theme of the fair, the board was free to work on the financial and administrative aspects of the project. In April, the World's Fair Legion, responsible for selling the $5.00 shares, was formally launched, and a Founder Members' drive, soliciting $1,000 from wealthy Chicagoans, was discussed but postponed amid reports of continuing antagonism toward the fair on the near North Side and in State Street businesses, two of the targeted areas for such a drive.[11]

By this time, the board had also discussed its relationship with union labor, wondering if an early request for support would oblige it later to employ only union members. In the end, union labor was widely utilized, but work stoppages and other labor problems were relatively insignificant.

Others were concerned about race relations, given the rapidly growing black community in Chicago. When Col. Stuyvesant Peabody, chairman of the Enrollment Committee, charged with fundraising, asked about the appointment of blacks to his committee, board member Robert R. McCormick suggested that they should not be ignored, but when it became clear that no one on the board had any close acquaintances in the black community, the idea was soon forgotten. The board officially adopted an anti-discrimination policy but, in keeping with the social attitudes of the time, made no positive efforts to involve black civic leaders in the exposition management. Similarly, there was little effort made to encourage black employment at the fair. A *Chicago Defender* reporter, Edgar Brown, and a delegation of blacks met with Dawes in January 1933 and apparently received some assurances that blacks would be considered for fair-related jobs, but the majority of black people who worked at the fair were restroom attendants who obtained their jobs because a black man was in charge of providing these employees. Altogether, perhaps 90 of the more than 5,200 Century of Progress employees were black.[12]

In May, the board fixed 1 June 1933, as the opening day for the fair, noting that in 1893 the World's Columbian Exposition had opened on 1 May and suffered poor attendance because of cold, rainy weather and the fact that schools were still in session. But the main focus of the board continued to be financial. Peabody announced a door-to-door drive to sell the $5.00 Legion shares in a campaign similar to wartime Liberty Loan drives. Initial response to this was disappointing, however, and the board attributed it to the recent and well-publicized failure of the 1926 Sesqui-Centennial Exposition in Philadelphia.[13]

By August, however, some 54,000 had enrolled in the Legion, contributing a total of $270,000, and Peabody announced that the house-to-house campaign would be replaced by approaches to employees of local plants and businesses. In addition, a fifty cents per week time payment plan would be made available.[14]

Nevertheless, more money was needed than could be raised by the $5.00 memberships in the World's Fair Legion. Although Founder's Memberships were being sold at $1,000 each, Dawes decided that until pledges amounting to $5 million were on hand, Congress should not be approached for its sanction, and the president should not be asked to invite foreign nations to participate. From the beginning, fair organizers wanted to avoid federal subsidization of the event and the experience that many past fair managers had faced of having to go back to Congress for 'remedial' appropriations.

Consequently, a new form of financing was devised. This was a $10 million bond issue, proposed by George Woodruff, and organized by Rufus Dawes's brother, Vice-President Charles G. Dawes. The bonds, known as gold notes, were to be secured by 40 per cent of the gate receipts of the fair as well as the individual guarantees of a number of private individuals. Pledges to guarantee these bonds came quickly in late 1928, however, the $5 million goal was reached, and on 5 February 1929, a joint resolution of Congress authorized President Herbert Hoover to invite foreign participation.[15]

In April 1929, the board created the position of general manager for the fair, and at Dawes's urging, hired Major Lenox Lohr, an army engineer and former editor of *Military Engineering* to fill the post. With him came Martha McGrew, his editorial assistant at *Military Engineer*, who now became his administrative assistant. Lohr and McGrew were an ideal team, and ran the day-to-day operations of the fair in a highly organized and business-like manner. After the stock market crash and onset of the depression, it was Lohr's steadfast sense of money management and McGrew's ability to be all things to all people that reined in the extravagance of the architects and decorators, kept the board of trustees on task, and found ways to cut costs and generate more income.[16]

In May, Samuel Insull, the Chicago utilities magnate, resigned as chairman of the General Finance Committee in order to try and salvage his crumbling business empire and was replaced by now former vice-president

Dawes. Although Dawes was about to leave for London to serve as Ambassador to the United Kingdom, his prestige and banking experience made his appointment a fortuitous one.

At its meeting in June 1929, the fair board, responding to a suggestion from a group of citizens, changed the name of the exposition from Chicago's Second World's Fair to the Century of Progress Exposition. This name, it was felt, reflected both the centennial celebration of the host city and the theme of progress through science.[17]

On 28 October 1929, the board, in dire need of cash, authorized the sale of the gold notes, and Charles G. Dawes quickly lined up pledges for over $6.6 million, of which just under $6 million was collected in ten calls for payment between January 1930 and October 1932. These infusions of capital were important in repaying early loans and in financing the construction costs of an Administration Building, thought necessary so that fair officials could be on the site and the $40,000 annual rent on their downtown office suite could be saved. In addition, the board wanted to have some popular exhibits open early to generate public interest and additional income. To this end, the members decided on a replica of Fort Dearborn, representing the Chicago of 1833, and a transportation exhibit, since few areas of science and technology had progressed further in the last hundred years.[18]

Following his successful effort to sell a majority of the gold bonds, Charles Dawes agreed to be one of three agents empowered to control disbursements from the bond sale and to make financial decisions in cases where the board did not have time or could not reach a decision. Dawes agreed, he wrote, because of his confidence in his brother 'Rufe.'

Dawes said that spending the $10 million must be done in ways that would raise still more money in order to complete the fair as planned. Echoing the board, he said that by the summer of 1931, a number of popular exhibits should be open to the public. At that time, Dawes hoped, the finance committee could approach the 10,000 corporations in Chicago for more bond purchases.[19]

Although the depression slowed considerably the pace of subscriptions to the bond issues, about $7.74 million in pledges had been received by June 1932, of which $6.11 million was paid in. This money had enabled the fair managers to build the Hall of Science, the Travel and Transport Building, and the Electrical Group, and make space available for industry to rent for their exhibits. The notion of having corporations, states, and other organizations pay for the use of exhibit space had first been suggested to the Century of Progress organizers in 1928 by Ernest T. Trigg, who had been on the staff of the Sesqui-Centennial Exposition in Philadelphia. At that time, planners were operating under the assumption that industrial exhibits would be put together co-operatively by trade associations, who were accustomed to paying for space at annual trade shows. The World's Columbian Exposition had offered free space, as had other past fairs, but this was no longer customary. The Century of Progress board adopted Trigg's suggestion, and the rental of exhibit space became the second largest source of income for the fair. When bond payments slowed in 1931 and 1932, the money received for exhibit space in one building was used to pay for the construction of the next building. The success of the Century of Progress in coaxing advance payment for space rental became an essential financial ingredient in completing the fair as planned by its opening day.[20]

Later the board would make a substantial amount of money from fees paid by concessionaires. Dr Forrest R. Moulton, the head of the concessions division, supervised the restaurants and amusements at the Century of Progress and devised a popular scheme whereby collection of royalties due the Century of Progress was deferred until the concessionaire had recouped most of his investment. Restaurants and amusements where an admission was charged generally paid the fair a percentage of their gross receipts, while other concessions were handled differently. For example, the delicately named Hump Hair Pin Manufacturing Company of Chicago received the concession to supply all hairpins sold in the twenty women's lounges on the fairgrounds. Under the terms of the agreement, Hump would provide 15,000 packages of ten-cent hairpins to the fair; they were to be sold in company-provided metal racks in the lounges, underneath a 28 inch by 42-inch advertising poster provided by the fair. The Century of Progress received $1,500 worth of hairpins; the Hump Hair Pin Manufacturing Company received $1,500 worth of advertising and the assurance that no other brand of hairpin would be sold at the fair. In a later day, Hump would doubtless advertise itself as 'the official hairpin of the Century of Progress.' In 1933, the fair received $3.02 million from concessions; in 1934, it received $3.8 million.[21]

Another important concern for the board was securing the site for the fair. Unlike the World's Columbian Exposition, when civic factions had battled for months over where to locate the fair before settling on Jackson Park, there was never any significant disagreement over using a site running from the Shedd Aquarium and Adler Planetarium at 12th Street south along the lakefront to 39th Street. This site included Northerly Island, which extended south from the planetarium to 23rd Street and created a lagoon between it and the mainland. When bisected by a bridge around 16th Street, the lagoon became in effect two lagoons, and allowed greater latitude in architectural planning and the scheduling of events.

This land was owned by the state of Illinois and was under the jurisdiction of the South Park Commission, an autonomous Chicago body charged with managing park land in the southern part of the city. In June 1929, the state legislature authorized the use of the land for the exposition, and on 16 April 1930, the park commission gave its permission to use the land to build an exposition that 'will open a new era in the exposition projects of the world.' The fair board had to see that the grounds were restored to their original condition after the close of the exposition and to pay a $1 million surety bond to guarantee compliance. At first, the park commissioners, led by Edward J. Kelly, who would be mayor of Chicago by the time the fair opened, wanted to influence the decisions made about the site. Kelly suggested filling in the north part of the lagoon and placing a number of exposition buildings in Grant Park, to the northwest of the site, a move that would place the aquarium, planetarium, and Field Museum of Natural History in the center of the fairgrounds. But the fair's board of trustees felt that Kelly's ideas were impractical (the lagoon was 40 feet deep) and expensive ($1 million had already been spent to landscape Grant Park). Subsequently, the park commission let the fair managers have their way in the development of the site.[22]

President Rufus Dawes made an extensive report to the board on the status of the fair on 7 May 1930, just about a year after serious planning had begun. He noted that a site plan and tentative layout had been completed, that working plans for the Administration Building were nearly done, that plans for the Travel and Transportation Building were in progress, and that final preliminary studies for two other exhibit buildings were also underway. He noted that Lenox Lohr had a staff of fifty-six working for him, and that the National Research Council's Science Advisory Committee was coming up with many ideas for exhibits and an overall 'science philosophy.' Finally, he reported that there had already been expressions of interest in participating in the Century of Progress from a number of foreign governments and foreign nationality groups in the United States.[23]

It was not until October 1930 that the oncoming global economic depression became a serious threat to the Century of Progress. On 1 October,

Dawes wrote to John Stephen Sewell, a member of Lohr's staff then traveling in Europe, that '[t]he extreme depression of feeling in the midst of these hard times will cause some delay in the collection of the call [for gold note payments] made on October 1. . . . [I]n the meantime, [we are] borrowing money for our necessities. I hope the economists are right in their hopeful predictions.'[24]

But as Dawes later explained in his *Official Report*, the depression did bring with it certain advantages. There was a ready and willing supply of labor that would work very cheaply. The board could buy supplies and equipment for less money and could negotiate cheaper contracts for services. For example, bids for the construction of the water and sewer systems came in at 15 per cent under estimates, indicating that contractors were looking for work to do, regardless of the profit margin. The depression also reduced the grandiose expectations the public might have had about a large world's fair, so that when the fair did open, it overwhelmed visitors by exceeding their pre-conceived notions.[25]

Still, the depression continued to take its toll on the fair and its workers until opening day. In March 1932, the Building Construction Employers' Association of Chicago, under whose wing most construction workers were hired, announced that wages would be cut approximately 20 per cent across the board. Common laborers would be paid $82\frac{1}{2}$ cents per hour, while skilled workers would be paid up to $1.42 per hour, depending on their particular craft. By 1932 also, the board of trustees was frequently paying its vendors or service providers part of what they were due in gold notes or admission tickets. For example, a 15 September 1932 contract with the Arthur Dixon Transfer Company for 'adequate and efficient trucking facilities' provided that 70 per cent of the contract price would be paid in gold notes or promissory notes (if by the time of payment all the gold notes had been subscribed to). Even Dawes took a portion of his pay in gold notes.[26]

Although comparisons with the World's Columbian Exposition were inevitable, Century of Progress managers spent a great deal of time and effort studying other fairs to see what could be learned from them. The records of the Century of Progress are filled with detailed descriptions of aspects of the fairs in St Louis (1904), San Francisco (1915), and Philadelphia (1926), ranging from daily attendance records to weather reports to financial information. In addition, official visits were made to virtually all of the fairs that took place in Europe in the late 1920s and early 1930s.

Helen M. Bennett, who became the assistant to Dr Fay Cooper-Cole, the director of the Social Sciences exhibit, had visited the Wembley Exhibition in Britain in 1925, as well as several smaller European fairs and submitted a report to the Chicago fair board in 1928. She noted that the Wembley fair, which had run two seasons (1924–25) had been unsuccessful because it had not been ready for its 1924 opening and was plagued by bad weather the following year. Moreover, it was a British Empire exhibition and the products and other exhibits on display were not varied enough. She also felt that there were not enough amusements nor attractions in Wembley itself, which is a rather distant suburb of London.

Lohr himself went to the annual Canadian National Exhibition in Toronto in August 1930 and learned much about what not to do. He was particularly appalled at the entertainment section – 'the midway border[s] on disgust,' but is still 'the best of these kind (sic) of traveling shows.' Well-patronized, it grossed over $250,000 during a two-week operation, and while Lohr could appreciate those numbers, he was pleased to note that the Canadian midway bore no resemblance to the planned Century of Progress 'Playland.'[27]

D. H. Burnham made a European trip in the fall of 1930 and visited the Liège and Antwerp fairs, and continued on to Paris to look over the site of the 1931 Colonial Exposition, then under construction. Several Century of Progress officials, including Burnham, visited the Paris fair in 1931 and learned much from it, particularly with regard to color, lighting, and night-time views. Although Burnham's diaries reveal him to be a rather stuffy individual, he was positively transfixed by the Paris fair, calling it an 'overpowering' success and the 'greatest exposition of all times.' He wrote a lengthy and detailed report on his observations, emphasizing those aspects of the fair that worked well for Parisian visitors and should be copied by the Century of Progress. He stressed the need to leave a good deal of space along waterways and in front of buildings to allow crowds to see attractions such as colored fountains and to move around relatively freely. He was greatly impressed with the replica of Angkor Wat, the ancient temple located in Cambodia, and felt that the Century of Progress should make the Maya Temple just as spectacular. Finally, Burnham was impressed with the French use of color at Paris, and the way in which the fair organizers there created 'picturesqueness,' in the foreign villages, with the colonial natives in their traditional dress, and even in such mundane things as restaurant table umbrellas. Following a lunch in London with Charles G. Dawes shortly after seeing the Paris fair, Burnham wrote in his diary, 'We must have strange music, exotic odors, and queer people – oriental, yellow and black in their native costumes milling around. Even if we have to dress up every nigger in Chicago that summer.'[28]

One of the principal responsibilities of the board of trustees beginning in 1930 was to arrange for federal, state, and foreign participation in the Century of Progress. Part of the rationale behind the European visits of Burnham and other fair officials was to generate interest among Europeans in the Century of Progress and induce foreign participation. In October 1930, Dawes and Sewell went to London to open a European office of the Century of Progress. Headed by Sir Henry Cole, an experienced exhibition manager, the London office publicized the Century of Progress and advised potential exhibitors. Fair officials were doubtless heartened in January 1931 when the recently approved International Convention on Expositions sanctioned participation by its members in the Century of Progress.

At the Paris Colonial Exposition in 1931, the Century of Progress put together a display that occupied a significant part of the United States pavilion. This exhibit consisted of a series of dioramas portraying different views of the United States; several were constructed for the pavilion by Century of Progress craftspeople and sent over to Paris, and then were later returned for display at the Chicago fair. Among the dioramas were five of Chicago, representing the city of 1833, of 1933, and of the future, as well as of North Michigan Avenue and of the planned Century of Progress site. C. Bascom Slemp, the United States Commissioner-General at the Paris fair, reported that the fair was attracting 150,000 visitors a day, and that the Century of Progress exhibit was a popular feature.[29]

The most peripatetic traveler on behalf of the Century of Progress was Dr Allen D. Albert, who functioned as a special assistant to Dawes and who made European trips in 1930 and 1931, and then journeyed to Japan and China for two months in the summer of 1932. Despite the fact that United States-Japanese relations were tense over the diplomatic crisis concerning Japan's recent takeover of Manchuria, the Japanese Diet authorized participation in the Century of Progress on 3 September. Although the nature of the Japanese exhibit had not been worked out, Albert was enthusiastic: 'I believe the Japanese exhibit will astonish America. It will reveal the New Japan, as reflected in the educational methods of the country.'[30]

Albert's fortune was equally good in China. He secured China's participation; the Chinese then engaged H. K. Murphy, an American architect living in Shanghai, to lay out a village on a one-acre site near the 18th

Street entrance. The village included a Chinese tea-garden, a typical home of a Chinese gentleman, a restaurant, an open-air theater, and craft shops.[31]

There was general agreement among Cole, Sewell, and other Century of Progress officials that foreign participation should take the form of the 'village' concept that had proven so popular in fairs dating back to the World's Columbian Exposition in 1893 and had impressed Burnham and other fair officials at the European fairs they had visited between 1929 and 1931. Although at the World's Columbian Exposition, the villages had been used for ethnological purposes, with the implicit objective of demonstrating the superiority of the Anglo-Saxon race, the villages of the later fairs, and ultimately the Century of Progress villages, generally represented more developed countries and were entertainment oriented. Thus, a particular country or region erected a cluster of houses reflecting the character and history of that place. The houses would portray various architectural styles and contain people in authentic costume doing representative arts and crafts work. There would be shops and restaurants, and perhaps a place where theatrical or musical events could be staged. A principal reason for encouraging villages was the fact that high United States tariffs militated against commercial exhibits that included the display of manufactured products. It was proposed, therefore, that foreign exhibits be so designed as to lure tourists from the United States to Europe. Some countries might also take part in the scientific or industrial exhibits; those with contributing scientists could place exhibits in the basic science displays in the Hall of Science; industrial exhibits, if suitable, might be accommodated in the appropriate pavilion. Although many countries wanted to construct a national pavilion, Sewell was confident that he could, in the end, convince them to build a village instead.[32]

As the worldwide depression deepened, Century of Progress officials were forced to adopt a more flexible policy with respect to foreign participation. In February 1931, Dawes advised Sewell that the fair would be as accommodating as possible in areas such as space allocation; in no case would a foreign nation be placed somewhere that would be disadvantageous to its interests. Moreover, foreign nations which want to participate in ways other than a village should be free to do so, despite the preference of the fair management for villages. In light of this, Louis Skidmore, head of the design section, suggested that a generic pavilion of a 'simple, dignified' style could be built for foreign nations at about twenty cents a cubic foot, including some landscaping. As an alternative, he proposed that preliminary designs could be prepared in the foreign country, or by ethnic groups from that country who were in the United States, and then sent to the Century of Progress for approval. Once approved, the actual contracting and construction supervision could be handled by exposition personnel, with perhaps one representative from the foreign nation.

In the end, only Belgium, among European nations, constructed a village in 1933; its success, as well as that of a more commercialized village-type attraction known as the Streets of Paris, led several others to do the same in 1934. A few countries, including Italy, Sweden, and Czechoslovakia, had traditional pavilions, while others installed their exhibits in a Hall of Nations that was located in the Travel and Transport Building. Some seventeen foreign governments were represented at the Century of Progress in 1933, although probably more than thirty had planned to participate before the depression forced them to abandon their plans.[33]

Federal and state participation was easier to arrange for. The commitment of the federal government had been assured in early 1929 when Congress had authorized President Hoover to invite foreign governments to participate. In June 1930, Congress passed a resolution for federal participation and appropriated $1.725 million for a building and exhibits. Hoover appointed a commission composed of high-ranking representatives from the State, Agriculture, and Commerce departments; its job was to determine what form federal participation should take. In February 1932, Congress reaffirmed the matter of the federal presence at the Century of Progress but cut the budget to $1 million. A US Commissioner, Harry S. New, a former governor of Indiana, was appointed to co-ordinate the details of constructing the US government building and installing the exhibits from the various government agencies that were participating. After the fair opened, New's job was to represent the government at ceremonial occasions. Much of the actual administrative work was done by Assistant Commissioner W. B. Causey, a World War I veteran and construction executive, and Assistant Secretary Edith Levy, who had held administrative assistant jobs at recent fairs in Philadelphia and Seville.[34]

In a departure from tradition, the board of trustees decided not to allow states, except for Illinois, to build their own pavilions, for fear they might be architecturally confusing and dissonant. States that wanted to participate would have to rent space in a fair-designed building. As Sewell put it, '[O]ld-fashioned state pavilions will merely clutter up the grounds without adding to the attractiveness of the Exhibition as a whole,' and, he added, so many small pavilions would also add considerably to the fair's overhead expenses. Sewell also discouraged the idea of states following the European 'village' idea as a way of promoting tourism, insisting that states would be far better off putting up attractive displays in the states' building.

Invitations were sent out to all states in December 1930, and most expressed their interest by appointing a commission. A special committee headed by Col. Christopher Van Deventer visited many states in 1931 to encourage participation, and for a time, it looked as if as many as forty states would participate. As the economic crisis worsened, however, more and more state legislatures could not or would not appropriate the funds needed. An elaborate Hall of States was built in conjunction with the Federal Building, but by the time the fair opened, only twenty-two states and Puerto Rico had installed exhibits there. Illinois, as the host state, built its own separate pavilion, the Illinois Host House, which included a reception room for visiting dignitaries.[35]

After 1930, the Century of Progress Board of Trustees had made most of its important decisions or had delegated them to the Architectural Commission, the Science Advisory Committee, or the Director of Works. The financial scheme of the fair was in place, the staff had moved into the Administration Building the past November, other buildings were well into the planning stage, and an active publicity department was churning out press releases. The board of trustees, or its executive committee, spent its meetings approving a multitude of contracts, taking care of personnel matters, and making decisions on the details of the fair, such as renaming the Temple of Science the Hall of Science, evidently to rid it of a religious connotation, and determining the scale of admission prices (fifty cents for adults, twenty-five cents for children, $15.00 for a season pass). A good deal of time was spent speculating on potential attendance figures, using the attendance of past fairs and a formula based on 'x' times the host city's population. The 'x' ranged from ten to twenty, and with the estimated 1933 population of metropolitan Chicago pegged at 5 million, most of the attendance projections were wildly optimistic.[36]

The attendance projections did not appear out of line on Opening Day, 27 May 1933, when almost 120,000 crowded in to see Postmaster General James A. Farley officially open the fair. The opening day had been changed from 1 June to 27 May in a vain effort to accommodate President Franklin Roosevelt's schedule, but the president found himself unable to attend, as did Vice-President John Nance Garner. Thus the honor fell to Farley.[37]

The inaugural day ceremonies had two parts. In the morning, there was a parade with 500 persons dressed in various native costumes and carrying the flags of forty nations, followed by an 11 a.m. ceremony featuring speeches by Rufus Dawes, Mayor Edward J. Kelly, and Farley, and the presentation of the Queen of the Century of Progress, Lillian Anderson, of Racine, Wisconsin. In an evening ceremony, visitors listened to a concert by the Chicago Symphony Orchestra and a 2,500-voice chorus and heard opera star Lawrence Tibbett sing the national anthem. Speeches were by Dawes and Edwin B. Frost, the director emeritus of the Yerkes Observatory, whose idea it was to have the fair lights activated by light from the star Arcturus, forty light years distant, thus providing a symbolic link between the two Chicago fairs. At 9.15 p.m., the Arcturus light was activated, the fair lights went on, and the Century of Progress Exposition was underway.[38]

Notes

1   Quoted in Cathy Cahan and Richard Cahan, 'The lost city of the depression,' *Chicago History*, IV, Winter 1976–77, p. 234.
2   Letter from Myron E. Adams to Mayor William E. Dever, 17 August 1923, reprinted as pamphlet, Chicago, 1926; *Chicago Tribune*, 27 May 1933. Adams died in 1930 and therefore never saw the outcome of his suggestion.
3   Rufus C. Dawes, *Report of the President of a Century of Progress to the Board of Trustees*, Chicago, 1936, p. 20; 'Chronology of early history,' Century of Progress Papers, Series 15, File 21, Department of Special Collections, University Library, University of Illinois at Chicago (hereafter referred to as COP 15–21).
4   Minutes of the meeting of the Board of Trustees, 21 May 1926 (hereafter referred to as Trustees' Meeting), COP 3–47.
5   *Chicago Daily News*, 28 June 1926.
6   'Chronology of early history,' COP 15–21; Trustees' Meeting, 13 December 1927, COP 3–46.
7   'Chronology of early history,' COP 15–21; Lenox R. Lohr, *Fair Management: The Story of a Century of Progress Exposition*, Chicago, 1952, p. 15.
8   Dawes, *Report of the President*, p. 39; C. G. Dawes dinner file, COP 9–32; 'Chronology of early history,' COP 15–21; *Chicago Tribune*, 17 June 1933. In July 1933, A Virginian, Edwin G. Decker, wrote to US Commissioner Harry S. New, complaining about the lack of coverage of the Century of Progress in the eastern press. New replied that in his view, the press office of the fair was 'exceedingly good,' and that the problem stemmed from the fact that editors of eastern papers did not believe the fair merited much attention. Century of Progress (COP) Papers, Record Group (RG) 43, Entry 1392, Box 12, US National Archives, Washington D.C.
9   Burnham to Charles Moore, 13 January 1928, COP 1–2371.
10 Century of Progress to Paul Cret, 2 February 1928, COP 5–9. This file contains copies of letters to each of the architects invited to join the commission, their replies, and

copies of the resolution setting out the responsibilities of the Architectural Commission. See also Trustees' Meeting, 2 March 1928, COP 3–44.

11   Trustees' Meeting, 25 April 1928, COP 3–44.

12   Trustees' Meeting, 23 March 1928, COP 3–44; August Meier and Elliott M. Rudwick, 'Negro protest at the Chicago world's fair, 1933–1934,' *Journal of the Illinois State Historical Society*, LIX, Summer 1966, pp. 161–71; Barbara Hart, 'An American dilemma on display: Black participation at the Chicago Century of Progress exposition, 1933–34,' *Report for the Chicago Urban League Research and Planning Department*, n.d.

13   Trustees' Meeting, 9 May 1928, COP 3–43.

14   Trustees' Meeting, 14 August 1928, COP 3–42.

15   'Chronology of early history,' COP 15–21; Telegram, Charles Dawes to Rufus Dawes, 8 December 1928, COP 9–29.

16   'Chronology of early history,' COP 15–21.

17   *Ibid.*; Lohr, *Fair Management*, p. 15.

18   Trustees' Meeting, 27 May 1929, COP 3–37 and 28 October 1929, COP 3–35; Lohr, *Fair Management*, pp. 31–32; Dawes, *Report of the President*, p. 49.

19   Charles Dawes to Rufus Dawes, 31 October 1929, COP 9–29.

20   Dawes, *Report of the President*, pp. 26–27; Daniel H. Burnham, 'How Chicago finances its exposition,' *Review of Reviews*, LXXXVI, October 1932, pp. 37–38.

21   Brooks Contracting Company to Sol Goldberg, 16 May 1933, COP 10–1265; Dawes, *Report of the President*, pp. 72–75.

22   'Chronology of early history,' COP 15–21; Digest of meeting held in Burnham studio, 5 August 1929, COP 5–40; Resolution, South Park Board, 29 October 1929, COP 9–32; Dawes, *Report of the President*, pp. 37–38.

23   Trustees' Meeting, 7 May 1930, COP 3–33.

24   Rufus Dawes to John Stephen Sewell, 1 October 1930, COP 9–33.

25   Dawes, *Report of the President*, pp. 49–51; 'History: physical layout,' COP 15–39. This series contains, among other things, Lohr's notes and chapter outlines for *Fair Management*.

26   List of revised wages, Building Construction Employers' Association, 10 March 1932, COP 11–22; Trustees' Meetings, November–December 1932, COP 3–20; Confidential Files, Rufus C. Dawes, COP 9–33. Dawes took no salary until June 1932, when he accepted a monthly salary of $1,000 in cash and $250 in gold notes. In July 1933, this was raised to $1,833.34 in cash and $250 in gold notes, or $25,000 per year. In November 1933, he refused the offer of a raise to $40,000 per year.

27   Helen M. Bennett, 'Report on current European fairs,' unpublished typescript, 1928?, COP 6–156; Lohr to Rufus Dawes, 2 September 1930, COP 9–33.

28   D. H. Burnham to Lohr, 6 November 1930, COP 1–2371; D. H. Burnham, 'Report on the Paris exposition of 1931,' Burnham Brothers Collection, Art Institute, Chicago (hereafter referred to as BBC); D. H. Burnham diary, 2 September 1931, BBC.

29   Sewell to Lohr, 8 October 1930; Trustees' Meeting, 29 October 1930, COP 3–32; Rufus Dawes to Sewell, 13 February 1931, COP 11–12; C. Bascom Slemp to Rufus Dawes, 6 July 1931, COP 1–8079; C. W. Fitch to Sewell, 8 January 1932, COP 1–8080; Slemp to Rufus Dawes, 24 February 1932, COP 1–8080; Louis Skidmore to Foreign Participation Section, 24 June 1932, COP 11–41. Henry Cole, the London representative of the Century of Progress, had been deeply involved with the management of the 1924–25 Wembley Exhibition and was associated with the English Overseas Trade Organization. He traveled on behalf of the Century of Progress, visited

other European fairs, and died in Spain on 28 September 1932. Dawes, *Report of the President*, p. 68.

30   Press Release, COP, 13 September 1932, COP 1–154.
31   Press Release, COP, 13 September 1932, COP 1–154. Albert's trip was sponsored by the Rotary Club; he had been president of Rotary International in 1915–16.
32   Sewell to Lohr, 6 October 1930, COP 11–11; Memorandum on foreign participation, COP 15–121.
33   Lohr, *Fair Management*, pp. 153–54; Final Report, US Commissioner, 1933, COP Papers, RG 43, Entry 1392, Box 6, National Archives. See also Digest of Federal, State, and Foreign Participants, COP 11–69.
34   Dawes, *Report of the President*, pp. 64–65; Digest of Federal, State, and Foreign Participants, COP 11–69; Edith Levy file, COP Papers, RG 43, Entry 1392, Box 8, National Archives. Levy was the administrative assistant to Commissioner New.
35   Trustees' Meeting, 12 August 1931, COP 3–29; Dawes, *Report of the President*, pp. 66–67; Sewell to Dawes, 21 October 1930; Sewell to Lohr, 2 February 1931.
36   Miltons Mayer, 'To the brave belongs the fair', *Vanity Fair, XXX*, April 1933, p. 20; R. McFarlan to C. Young, 7 November 1930, COP 6–166. Trustees' Meeting, 5 February 1931, COP 3–31. The ten-member executive committee consisted of Rufus Dawes, Britton I. Budd, D. H. Burnham, Abel Davis, Mrs Kellogg Fairbank, Amos Miller, Dr Forrest R. Moulton, Charles S. Peterson, Dr William Allen Pusey, and George Woodruff.
37   *Chicago Tribune*, 17–19 May and 29 May 1933.
38   *Chicago Tribune*, 18 May and 26–27 May 1933.

5   Building a Century of Progress

> The fair stands as a symbol of the architecture of the future – the icons of the past cast aside, the ingenuity of the designers of the present thrown on their own resources to meet the problems of the day[1]

> I look on the architecture of the Century of Progress as a definite retrogression, a reversal of a fine tendency and a return to the regrettable aberrations of the fifty years of esthetic dark ages in the United States. . . . [T]hese buildings at Chicago will prove not only a revelation but [also] a warning.[2]

From the beginning, it was clear to all concerned with the Century of Progress that the fair's architecture would be highly distinctive and reflective of the theme of scientific progress. Mindful of the architectural success of the World's Columbian Exposition and aware that a committee of leading national architects had designed the buildings for that fair, the Century of Progress board chose to follow the same course and appoint an architectural commission composed of architects from both Chicago and other parts of the country.

In March 1928, the board appointed five architects: Harvey Wiley Corbett, Raymond Hood, and Ralph T. Walker of New York; Paul Philippe Cret of Philadelphia; and Arthur Brown, Jr., of San Francisco. These five, in turn, added three Chicago architects to the commission: John A. Holabird, Edward H. Bennett, and Hubert Burnham, the latter a son of Daniel H. Burnham, the Chicago architect who as Chief of Construction for the World's Columbian Exposition, had co-ordinated the spectacular architecture of that fair. Later, Joseph Urban, the color consultant, and Ferrucio Vitale, the landscape director, were added to the commission, and another Burnham son, Daniel H., Jr., attended most of the commission meetings as the representative of the board of trustees until he was named Director of Works in October 1929. Dr Allen D. Albert, Dawes's special assistant, was honorary secretary of the commission.[3]

There was some controversy over the exclusion of Frank Lloyd Wright from the architectural commission. Although his career had been in something of an eclipse for a decade or more, Wright was still arguably America's greatest living architect, as well as a major international proponent of modernism in architecture. At a public meeting in New York in March 1931, the noted social critic Lewis Mumford, who remembered Louis Sullivan's relegation to a relatively minor role at the World's Columbian Exposition, deplored the fact that Wright had not been invited to join the Century of Progress's architectural commission. Wright himself said that he was trying to 'bring architecture back to America as something real to America,' but that the proposed Century of Progress architecture was a 'sham,' and 'only bad theater where theater does not belong.' Commission member Raymond Hood, who could not have enjoyed hearing the comments of Mumford and Wright, acknowledged that Wright was a great architect but had not been invited to join the commission because he was 'too much of an individualist. Since the affair is to be built by a commission, I can not see how one with such individual ideas as Mr. Wright could work with it. . . . [I]t would be too difficult to harness Mr. Wright to our ideas.'[4]

The commission met three or four times a year for two or three days at a time between 1928 and early 1932, usually in Chicago. After 1932, with most of the major architectural decisions made and with the economic constraints of the depression forcing the elimination of many of the most extravagant and creative ideas, the commission delegated much of the routine work to a sub-committee composed of the three Chicago architects, and to Louis Skidmore, who was the fair's chief of design. At the opening of the fair, 27 May 1933, the commission held one final meeting and disbanded.

At their first meeting, 23–25 May 1928, the commissioners chose Corbett as chairperson, took a plane ride over the prospective site, agreed to create a composite design for the exposition, and most importantly, adopted a statement of architectural principle, in which they stated their intention to reflect in their designs the development of architecture in the world since 1893, including new modes of construction, new inventions, and advances in the use of artificial lighting. In addition, given the lakefront site of the fair, the commissioners agreed to maximize the use of water as a design feature. At this time, with the country still in the full bloom of prosperity, the architects conceived of a fair of great extravagance, one in which each of them could create an architectural masterpiece on the order (but not the style) of the architecture of the World's Columbian Exposition.[5]

It is notable that the commissioners took on the task of designing the buildings for the Century of Progress as a purely professional activity, for which they expected to be well paid. Initially, they recommended to the board of trustees that they be paid $50 per day while working for the Century of Progress, plus expenses for attending meetings. Beginning in January 1930, when the exposition had been capitalized to the extent that it was certain to occur, the architects negotiated for themselves a $5,000 yearly retainer plus a commission of $1\frac{1}{2}$ per cent of the cost of construction of buildings they designed, the commissions to be pooled and divided equally among all eight architects. Finally, an amount equal to 75 per cent of the commission total would be charged to the board to cover overhead. There is no record that the board seriously balked at paying these fees, which totaled some $63,623.72, even when the depression tightened the fair's financial situation, and by all accounts, the architectural commission, the board of trustees, and the general manager's office all co-operated remarkably well.[6]

Working only from their own statement of principles, a general sense of the theme of the exposition, and a site map, the architects decided at their second meeting in December 1928 to place the main entrance at 23rd Street, near the longitudinal center of the site. There was considerable discussion about the advantages and disadvantages of erecting permanent buildings for the fair, based on a report that Allen Albert had prepared. Ultimately, the architectural commission heeded Albert's argument that any permanent structure built on the site had to conform to 'park purposes,' defined as 'recreation and amusement,' and that it would be nearly impossible to convert such a building as a hall of science into something that would conform to the park board's requirement. Moreover, any permanent building would have to win the approval of the fair management, the park board, and the financial backers of the project.

The commissioners also sensed that previous fairs had covered too much area, contributing to visitor fatigue, and therefore thought it important to consider designing multi-story buildings in order to concentrate exhibits. Linked to this notion was the concept of using moving sidewalks or other mechanical means to bring people on to the site and into the exposition buildings, perhaps even at the upper stories of the buildings.[7]

There was general agreement that the commission should plan for about five million square feet of exhibit space, equal to that of the World's Columbian Exposition, that the Fine Arts exhibit should be housed in the Art Institute, about a mile away, with shuttle transportation provided, and that building design should emphasize economical and fireproof construction. The commissioners reiterated their intent to maximize the use of artificial illumination and water, and concluded that automobiles had no place on an exposition site.

The board of trustees met with the architects for the first time on 7 December. They heard the preliminary plans and concepts and concluded that they were 'properly imaginative and bold,' without losing sight of the practical needs of the fair.[8]

In a series of meetings in 1929, the Architectural Commission continued to try and flesh out their initial principles and ideas. The architects continued to give strong consideration to multi-storied buildings and wondered about such niceties as fire safety and foundation materials. There was general agreement that the exposition ought to have some sort of 'colossal thing,' in Holabird's words, that would probably be vertical and would offer opportunities for creative light and water treatment.

In a meeting of the commission in January, Paul Philippe Cret presented a conceptualization of the site that came to underlie much of the planning that followed. The long, narrow geography of the site precluded visualizing it as a single unit, he argued, so it must be seen as three separate but related units. The area around the main entrance at 23rd Street would be the central focus of the fair, and the areas north and south of the main entrance would be the other two units. After hearing Cret's conceptualization, the commission agreed that the nature of the site dictated a major axis running parallel to the lakeshore and a minor axis perpendicular to it and extending across the site from the main entrance to the lake. The commission also agreed that there should be additional entrances north and south of 23rd Street.[9]

After discussion during the summer and early fall as to how to proceed with the actual design of the major exposition buildings, the commission agreed that the site should be divided among the several members of the commission, with each architect being responsible for the design of buildings within his sector. It was made clear that there would be no distinctive 'style' of architecture, as there had been for the major buildings of the World's Columbian Exposition, and that the entire commission would review and approve the designs of each architect to ensure an overall architectural harmony.

With those principles established, the commission met in late October 1929 and assigned sectors and buildings to each architect. The Hall of Science, arguably the most important building of the fair, went to Holabird.

Ralph Walker was given the signature tower, the bridges across the lagoon, and the area at the south end of the island. Edward Bennett was to design the area around the north lagoon and the water court, while Hubert Burnham would handle the 23rd Street entrance and the buildings south of it. The area in between the science building and the 23rd Street entrance was the responsibility of Corbett, and a court section west of the science building was given to Cret. Arthur Brown received the north end of the island, nearest the planetarium, an area that was likely to include the state exhibit buildings and a theater group. Finally, Raymond Hood was to design a casino and other buildings east of the science group. Left out of this mix were the Administration Building, designed by Holabird & Root, Hubert Burnham, and Edward Bennett, the plans for which were already well under way, and the Travel and Transport Building, due to open to the public in 1931. To help co-ordinate all of this, the commission recommended the appointment of Daniel H. Burnham, Jr., as Director of Works, a recommendation that the board of trustees readily accepted.[10]

By this time, the $10 million initial capitalization of the Century of Progress was assured, and the architects were anxious to know what percentage was available for buildings. C. W. Farrier, serving as acting Director of Works and later to become Burnham's assistant, told the commission that some $5.5 million would be available for the first phase of building, after site preparation and engineering work. The commissioners were dubious that much could be done with this sum of money, particularly

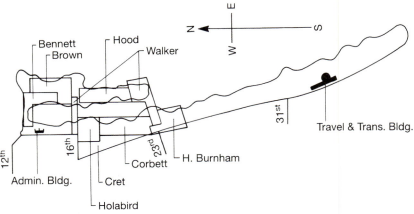

14 Space allocation for architects, 1929. Century of Progress Exposition.

considering all the construction that was going on in the nearby Loop. Holabird groused that $100 million rather than $10 million would have to be spent to build an impressive fair that would not be overshadowed by the Loop's buildings.

Burnham reminded the architects that a more pressing problem was the board's insistence that a transportation exhibit be ready for the public by 1931. The commission agreed to let the Chicago members study the question and report back to the board as soon as practicable. This was the 'key to the fair,' said Holabird, and Hood added that it should be a 'very unusual' structure and that it should be located near the south end of the site to balance the Administration Building at the north end.[11]

By February 1930, the plans for the Administration Building had been approved and made public, and the initial response was hardly encouraging. Rufus Dawes's daughter Meg, a student at Vassar, wrote in despair, 'And honestly Mother are they going to erect that hideous thing for the Administration Building? I have had five Chicago people come weeping to me about it – it looks like a factory or public school. I hate that too plain modern stuff. I bet it will look as funny in twenty years as the Mid-Victorian stuff does now.' 'I have no idea of suggesting any change,' wrote father Dawes to Lohr.[12]

With the major sectors and buildings assigned to the various architects, the commission could turn its attention to some of the more detailed aspects of the fair. Discussion continued about transportation on the fairgrounds and the movement of visitors through multi-storied buildings. The Yellow Cab Company and the Chicago Motor Coach Company had given their blessing to a ground transportation scheme drawn up in Edward Bennett's office, and fanciful ideas about elevated transportation led to an agreement that pedestrian walkways or moving sidewalks could be built at an elevation of 47 feet, and elevated mechanical transportation could run at a height of 41 feet. These plans, however, were among the first items to be scrapped when the realities of the economic crisis became apparent in late 1930.[13]

In a commission meeting 19–21 May 1930, the architects' attention was turned to landscaping and, for the first time, color. Ferrucio Vitale, now a full member of the commission, urged the creation of a landscape committee and the making of prior arrangements with nurseries so that trees and shrubs would be available when needed along with men and equipment to plant them. Joseph Urban, a well-known stage set designer, was approved as a consultant to the commission and was asked to make color studies of the Administration and Travel and Transport Buildings. As the depression cut into the funding available for constructing extravagant buildings, Urban's color schemes became increasingly more important as the principal decorative element for the buildings of the Century of Progress.[14]

The growing awareness of the depression's impact was seen in small changes ordered as early as the spring of 1930: a music hall was eliminated, plans to develop the bathing beach area were held in 'abeyance,' and a permanent convention hall was to be consigned to an independent contractor. Among the architects, Raymond Hood was the one most bothered by the economic crisis. His principal responsibility was the Electrical Group, a large structure fronting on the lagoon across from the Hall of Science. In early 1930, when it was decided that this would be one of the earlier construction projects, Hood drew up plans that called for a waterfall to cascade down the lagoon side of the building. It was elaborate and expensive, but it tied the building, which also had an entrance from the lagoon, more fully into the water and satisfied one of the architectural principles.

Others on the architectural commission were less certain that Hood's waterfall justified its cost, and this sentiment was echoed by Lohr and the fair management, which suggested that much the same effect could be accomplished more inexpensively through the use of artificial lighting. A two-year battle ensued between Hood and the fair officials. In September 1930, Carl Lindefield, who worked in Hood's New York office, wrote Louis Skidmore that Hood 'is determined to try and bring the water back . . . , that the electrical display alone will be too mechanical and inclined towards a cheap looking arrangement.' In July 1931, with construction about to begin, Farrier reminded Hood that his building was already $48,500 over budget because of $75,000 worth of sculpture that was to be part of it. Farrier thought the deficit could be made up in other ways, but the implication with respect to the waterfall was clear. But not to Hood, however, who wrote back to Farrier in October, 'My main feeling is that before the fair is open we will see so damn many electrical gadgets and effects that water will have, as a foil against them, a wonderful impression, at least in this spot.'

The battle continued into 1932. In May, D. H. Burnham wrote Hood that economic reasons dictated the replacement of his waterfall with 'Mr. Tillson's electrical rocket.' Hood replied that this substitution would give the building a 'cheap Coney Island effect' and probably would not save any money in any case, but Burnham responded that the rocket would cost $5,000, as against the waterfall's $20,000, at a time when $75,000 had already been spent on 'sculptural embellishments' for the Electrical Group. The building was completed in April 1932 without a waterfall (or an electrical rocket) but with the most elaborate sculptural treatment of any exposition building as well as an impressive lighted fountain in the center court that was visible from the lagoon. The usually impassive Lenox Lohr called it a 'spectacle of superb beauty.'[15]

The depression also undermined plans for a signature structure for the fair, an assignment that had originally been given to Ralph A. Walker, although others had indulged in the fantasy, including the H. J. Heinz Company, which had wanted to build a 1,000-foot long pickle. Walker had envisioned a tower rising from the south lagoon on the minor axis created by the 23rd Street entrance, and thus, nearly at the center of the exposition grounds. Known as the Tower of Water and Light, this was to be a steel-framed structure 250 feet tall, decorated with 'giant fins and baffles' and covered with an exterior gypsum board product. It would have elevators installed to take visitors to various observation points, and there would be a 5,000 square foot exhibit hall in the base, with a ceiling 75 feet high. Water would be pumped to the top of the tower and allowed to cascade down the sides, creating a waterfall that would be particularly impressive when lit by floodlights at night. The Montgomery Ward Company was in line to underwrite the cost of this tower, and the US Gypsum Company was to provide the exterior gypsum board. Walker also considered a variation of this tower, one built entirely of steel and steel alloys and rising 450 feet out of the lagoon, with the same fins, baffles, and waterfall. Plans for the smaller tower remained under active consideration until the spring of 1932, when Montgomery Ward apparently withdrew its offer to finance the structure, and the commission turned instead to the Sky-Ride.[16]

The project that became the Sky-Ride was first suggested to fair officials by an engineer named William L. Hamilton in the summer of 1931. He described a 'scheme of travel' involving cars suspended between two high towers and traveling on a track or wire from one to the other. Fair officials were interested and discussed the idea with Hamilton but were unable to come to any definite plans to build it. The idea was not forgotten, however, and in the spring of 1932, with the planned Walker tower about to be abandoned, N. A. Owings, Louis Skidmore's deputy in the design area and the individual charged with obtaining in-kind donations from business, made arrangements with various contractors and suppliers to have it built. Owings, a self-styled 'wide-ranging predator,' got donations of the foundation work, the structural steel, the elevators, the suspension system, and the so-called 'rocket cars.'

Although contracts were signed in June 1932, the first steel was not placed until December, and the major part of the work had to be done in bad weather during the early months of 1933. A labor dispute caused further delays, and although the observation towers were finished by opening day, 27 May, the rocket cars were not installed, and their operation did not begin until 16 June. The Sky-Ride was impressive, however. The two towers, nicknamed 'Amos' and 'Andy' after the popular radio characters of the day, were 628 feet high and were located 1,850 feet apart on either side of the lagoon near 16th Street. Along with the bridge that crossed the lagoon at that point, the Sky-Ride helped to define the lagoon as two separate entities. The west tower stood between the stadium and the Hall of Science, while the east tower rose slightly north of the Electrical Group. The rocket cars traversed the distance between the towers at a height of 219 feet; a one-way trip took slightly more than three minutes. Although the Sky-Ride was architecturally out of scale and startlingly incongruous with the rest of the Century of Progress, visitors liked it and it remained among the most popular attractions during the two years of the fair.[17]

In one other important respect, however, the depression served a very positive purpose. It forced the architects to focus much more clearly than they might otherwise have on one of their original principles, the construction of economical buildings. By turning what appeared to be a setback into an advantage, the architects were able to create a significance for their work that went beyond the design elements they utilized. A December 1931 press release noted that rather than repeat the classical architectural models as had been done in 1893, the Century of Progress buildings would have a new beauty of their own and would suggest to builders opportunities in the use of new materials and techniques, including suspended roofs, as in the Travel and Transport Building, and prefabrication, as in the Administration Building.[18]

As construction got underway on most of the major buildings in 1931 and 1932, it was the Department of Works, headed by Daniel H. Burnham and Clarence W. Farrier, that bore the primary responsibility to economize on building costs. This involved the application of two principles: the efficient use of labor, and the utilization of lightweight materials to lessen the amount of structural steel and foundation work that would be needed. On-site labor, which tended to be expensive, could be substantially reduced by the use of prefabricated trusses, wall sections, and the like; moreover, the very nature of their prefabrication meant that they would be lightweight in order to facilitate their shipment and installation on the site.

Three other factors contributed to the success of this cost-cutting effort. First, the Century of Progress buildings were meant to be temporary buildings, as are most exposition buildings. This allowed experimentation in both design and construction that would not have been possible in a permanent building. Second, the nature of the site made formal building arrangements impossible and permitted a mix of 'small-area masses' raised to substantial heights and long, low buildings. The freedom of an asymmetrical site plan also allowed for creative cost-cutting. Finally, the fact that the Century of Progress was exempt from the provisions of Chicago's building code presented additional opportunities for experimentation.[19]

The major fair buildings were constructed for about sixteen cents per cubic foot, about one-sixth the cost of conventional commercial construction. Burnham and Farrier were the first to admit that the building methods employed at the Century of Progress could not be totally transferred to ordinary construction. But certain principles could be employed to cut costs on small buildings or residences based on a fifteen-year life span. Methods akin to those used at the exposition should produce buildings that would last that long, and owners should be able to amortize the cost of these buildings at a lower rate over fifteen years than they could for more permanent buildings designed to last more than twenty years. Even skyscrapers of the future could benefit from the legacy of the Century of Progress, wrote Burnham. The tall building of the future will be built of lightweight, unornamented, prefabricated sections and will cost thirty cents per cubic foot rather than the current seventy-five cents. Such buildings will have a useful life of about twenty years, governed by the serviceability of elevators, plumbing, and other 'fixtures.' These buildings will have virtually no windows, and what ornamentation there is will be carried out by lighting and color. Further expenses will be saved by having the framework bolted together for easy demolition. Such efficient, low-cost commercial structures, Burnham concluded, will stabilize business districts and land values and allow workers to live and work in more healthful and comfortable surroundings.[20]

When the Century of Progress opened on 27 May 1933, visitors saw a fair architecture that sharply contrasted with that of the World's Columbian

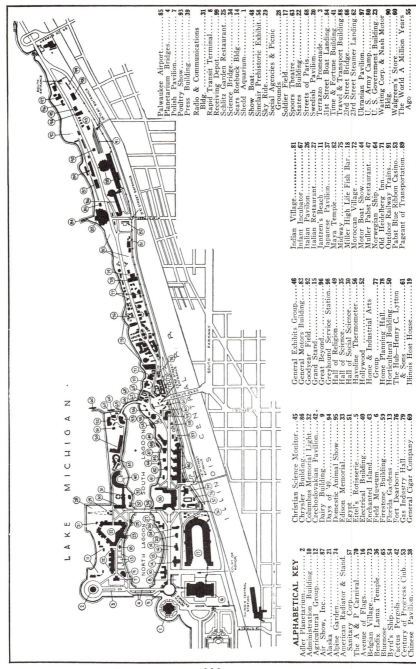

15 Site plan of A Century of Progress Exposition, 1933.

Exposition. There was no attempt to bring uniformity to building size, cornice height, or color, but there was a general similarity in the architectural style. As Daniel Burnham, Jr., put it, 'At least we shall not bore the public with a monotonous repetition of past patterns. . . . We frankly discarded the classical style with its balanced groupings of buildings around a court . . . [and] we turned our architects loose. . . . [O]ur celebration calls for an architecture in step with the tempo of the modern age.' Harvey Wiley Corbett was somewhat less enthusiastic, noting that '[the purpose of the architecture was] to house the exposition in the most effective and expeditious way, taking into account the conditions.'[21]

Whatever the rationale, the Century of Progress was dressed in 'modern' architecture, based on the precepts basic to Art Deco or Art Moderne, seen primarily in Europe during the 1920s at the Paris Decorative Arts Exposition of 1925, in the German Bauhaus, in the work of Dutch architects of the De Stijl movement, and more recently in the architecture seen at the 1930 Gothenburg Exposition in Sweden and the 1931 Colonial Exposition in Paris.[22]

But this was not the 'nit-picking, fussy' Art Moderne style currently in vogue in Europe or utilized in New York City's heralded Chrysler Building. Principally because of cost considerations, the use of new types of building materials, and the temporary nature of the buildings, this was a plainer, less elegant modern architecture, lacking much (but certainly not all) of the intricate geometry and stylistic bas-relief sculpture seen elsewhere. This variation of Art Deco, which has also been called 'Stripped Classicism,' had already been seen in such projects as the Rockefeller Center in New York (begun in 1931) and in the *Chicago Daily News* building (1928–29).

The architecture also complemented the movement of industrial designers into streamlining and the use of new materials, such as Bakelite (an early form of plastic), glass bricks, and Formica, that did not lend themselves to ornamentation. So it was left to Joseph Urban's intense and varied color scheme and the wide array of incandescent and gaseous tube lighting to substitute for more conventional kinds of ornamentation and provide the Century of Progress with a distinctiveness that fair visitors loved and architectural critics frequently dismissed as trivial and tawdry.[23]

With the exception of the Travel and Transport Building, all of the major theme pavilions of the Century of Progress were clustered around the lagoon. From the Shedd Aquarium and Adler Planetarium, pre-existing buildings which anchored the fair's northern end, fair buildings lined either side of the water from 12th Street down to the southern end of Northerly Island at 23rd Street, where a bridge connected the island with the mainland and the principal entrance to the site.

On the mainland side of the lagoon, visitors walked past the Administration Building, down a wide boulevard called the Avenue of Flags, to the Hall of Science, followed by the long, low General Exhibits Building, really five pavilions in one. On the island side of the water was the imposing US Government Building and Hall of States, followed by the Agricultural Building and the Electrical Group. Scattered here and there were smaller pavilions, built by sponsoring corporations, foreign countries, or commercial enterprises. From the 23rd Street entrance, visitors had to walk about eight blocks south, through the midway and its entertainment venues as well as the housing exhibit, to get to the transportation complex, dominated by the Travel and Transport Building. Nearby were the large pavilions of General Motors and Chrysler (Ford would join the fair in 1934), the smaller pavilions of Nash and Firestone, and the Maya Temple, where some of the social science exhibits were housed.

Of the major fair buildings, by far the most distinctive were the Hall of Science and the Travel and Transport Building. The Hall of Science, the principal 'theme' pavilion of the fair, was a 400 by 700-foot structure in the shape of a 'U' built on the west side of the lagoon at the 16th Street entrance. The court formed by the inside of the 'U' occupied 130,000 square feet and could hold up to 80,000 people. The dominant exterior feature was a 175-foot high tower at the southwest corner of the building. Inside, the principal space was the 'Great Hall of Science,' 260 feet long by 60 feet wide, with a 50-foot high ceiling; most of the rest of the interior was subdivided into standard exhibit space for the many pure science exhibits arranged by the Science Advisory Committee and its sub-committees.

The Travel and Transport Building consisted of two rather distinct parts: a cylindrical tower 125 feet high by 206 feet across, and a low exhibition hall connected to the back of the tower and extending about 700 feet to the north and 300 feet to the south. The cylindrical tower design derived from the need to have a large open space in which to place a large steamship exhibit as well as a display of locomotives and their development. Building this space in the nature of a locomotive roundatable was the ideal situation, and the high ceiling afforded by the dome allowed for dramatic lighting effects.

A dome of such size held up by steel trusses was problematical because of the great weight involved over such a span. So engineers came up with the idea of a suspended roof hung from cables that were installed along exterior columns. The dome itself was suspended from a network of crossing cables by short steel rods. The exterior walls of the building were the flat sides of channel steel sheets, primed and ready for painting. The total cost of the building came to about $800,000, or some seven and one-fourth cents per cubic foot.[24]

Scattered throughout the fairgrounds were hundreds of smaller structures and fixtures, some purely decorative, others utilitarian. The exposition staff called them 'gadgets,' for want of a better term, and they included kiosks, public restrooms and shelters, flags and flagpoles, lighting fixtures, benches, and trash receptacles. Generally, these were simple, unornamented devices, in keeping with the architectural simplicity of the fair's major buildings.

Some of the gadgets themselves were important and popular additions to the fair. Chief among these was the Havoline thermometer, a 240-foot high tower located near the 23rd Street entrance. The tower had temperature gradations and a tube filled with what appeared to be red liquid that accurately told the temperature. The actual thermometer mechanism, however, was located in the base of the tower; from it, signals were sent to illuminate one or more of a series of gaseous tubes in the tower to indicate the temperature. Another gadget, purely decorative, was the arrangement of four electric trees, 100 feet tall, located in the court of the Electrical Group. These trees were made of wire lath over a steel frame. The lath was covered with plaster and made to look like formally trimmed trees seen in Italian gardens. Special lighting heightened the effect.

Some gadgets never were built, often because a sponsor could not be found. Looking for an eye-catching device for the 12th Street entrance, staff designers sketched a 'Hoot-Nanny,' an open, spherical structure, 85 feet high, built around a central core, and set up over a fountain with colored lighting effects, but it was never built. Those gadgets that were built, large and small, served as the connecting tissue of the exposition, filling in empty spaces and leading visitors from one major building or activity center to the next.[25]

'Architecture is on its way, but whither is it going?' wrote Arthur F. Woltersdorf in *American Architect*. It was new, it was intriguing, it was distinctive, this Century of Progress architecture, but most contemporary critics were not quite certain how to evaluate it. Some older critics, such

16 The Hall of Science was the most important of the Century of Progress exhibit buildings, since its exhibits represented the principal theme of the fair. It was designed by Paul Philippe Cret and dominated the west shore of the lagoon.

17 Hall of Science, Century of Progress.

18 Designed by John A. Holabird, Edward H. Bennett and Hubert Burnham, the Travel and Transport Building was the most innovative structure at the Century of Progress Exposition, although many critics were distressed by its unconventional appearance.

19 Designed by Raymond Hood, the Electrical Group stood on the east shore of the lagoon and was the only major Century of Progress building accessible by boat.

20 The US Government Building (also referred to as the Federal Building) was located on Northerly Island, just to the north of the Electrical Group. Designed by Edward H. Bennett, it featured three 150-foot pylons representing each of the branches of the federal government.

21 One of the smaller exhibit buildings at the Century of Progress, the Dairy Building contained popular exhibits promoting dairy products and a dairy restaurant.

22 The Administration Building housed the official headquaters for the World's Fair Staff, end the Board of Trustees.

as Royal Cortissoz of the *New York Herald Tribune*, a self-styled 'traditionalist,' thought the Century of Progress architecture 'merely deplorable,' marking a real decline from 1893. He found little to like about the fair. The general plan was 'sprawling incoherence,' the color scheme was 'raw and repellent,' and overall, the effect was 'strained, odd, unlovely, and worst of all, almost incredibly uninteresting.'[26]

A. M. Frankfurter, writing in *Fine Arts*, also criticized the site plan for its lack of integration and organization and felt that the major exhibit buildings could have been more dignified and less pretentious. Woltersdorf thought that the buildings 'look[ed] like the pasteboard containers that they [were],' although he gave passing marks to the Hall of Science and the US Government Building for their 'architectural quality and proportion of parts.' Other critics were more charitable, recognizing the realities of the depression and the temporary nature of exposition buildings. A column in the *Architect and Engineer* acknowledged these factors but still maintained that the Century of Progress did not represent any sense of architectural progress since the World's Columbian Exposition.[27]

Eugene H. Klaber, who worked with the Century of Progress housing exhibit, reviewed the fair architecture for the *American Magazine of Art*. He, too, noted the temporary nature of fair buildings and how fairs were widely recognized as laboratories for architectural experimentation; fair buildings are often 'studies in form for the interest in form itself,' rather than totally functional buildings. Klaber rejected Burnham's assertion that new structural materials and methods would be a primary legacy of the Century of Progress. There were major difficulties in keeping the sheets of gypsum wallboard from expanding at their joints and twisting, and such material would never do for permanent buildings. Similarly, the light steel framework supporting the exposition buildings was nothing really new and would never be suitable for buildings meant to last more than the lifetime of a fair.

Klaber joined other critics in his dislike of the lack of a formal site plan, like the Court of Honor at the World's Columbian Exposition. He suggested that no study of the interrelationship between the buildings had been done, and that no attempt had been made to utilize the lagoon as a focal center, perhaps because it was too wide. But if there had been a sense of rationality in the layout, the Sky-Ride, with its high towers, would have destroyed it by ruining the sense of scale.[28]

Most of the favorable commentary was focused on individual buildings. Klaber, for example, liked the Agricultural Building, which he thought well-proportioned and well decorated by flagpoles, terraces, and railings. He also praised the Hall of Science for the good use made of the relationship with the lagoon and the fact that 'all sides [had] been designed,' in contrast to the Electrical Group and the Firestone Building, whose backs or sides were left in a 'crude' state.[29]

Among all the major fair buildings, the Chrysler Building received the most praise. Even Cortissoz, who liked very little about the Century of Progress, thought that the Chrysler Building was successful. In an unsigned article, the *Architectural Forum* reviewed the Chrysler Building, designed by Holabird and Root, and concluded that it could be the greatest contribution of the fair to modern architecture. The *Forum* was impressed with the spread out design of the building, the way the pylons were incorporated into the design, and the manner in which the building related to the nearby Travel and Transport Building.

In a sense, the architecture of the Century of Progress may be seen as an architecture of transition. Woltersdorf may have been on the mark when he wrote that the Century of Progress reflected the life and times of the 1920s, symbolized by lipstick, the hip flask, and the cocktail shaker; it 'expresses psychologically a passing era.' The raw modernism of the buildings and the bright colors used to paint them seemed to combine with the carnival spirit present in all expositions to recreate a mood that had disappeared with the stock market crash. At the same time, however, the architecture of the fair did serve to popularize modernism in America. It contributed its share to the blossoming of domestic and commercial architecture based in Art Deco and what was becoming known as the International Style, and to the trend in industrial design of streamlining, seen in everything from locomotives to toasters. And despite the claims of some critics, the use of new building materials and the emphasis on prefabrication left their marks on American building techniques, even if skyscrapers did not evolve into temporary buildings with a twenty-year life span. That the New York World's Fair of 1939–40 adopted a very similar architectural style is ample testament to the architectural legacy of the Century of Progress.[30]

Notes

1   'Branding the buildings at the Chicago fair,' *Literary Digest*, CXVI, 12 August 1933, p. 14.
2   *Ibid.*

Chicago's great world's fairs

3   Rufus C. Dawes, *Report of the President of a Century of Progress to the Board of Trustees*, Chicago, 1936, pp. 36–37.

4   *New York Times*, 26 February 1931; *Time*, 9 March 1931; John Cawelti, 'America on display: the world's fairs of 1876, 1893, 1933,' in F. C. Jaher (ed.), *The Age of Industrialism in America*, New York, 1968, pp. 355–56. Three months earlier, Bruce Bliven, editor of the *New Republic*, had written to Corbett about Wright's apparent exclusion from the Architectural Commission, noting that 'the action seems as incomprehensible as it is deplorable. If the report is correct, we shall want to criticise it in the *New Republic* as vigorously as we know how.' John Holabird replied to Bliven that Wright had always been 'favorably considered' and would be given some as yet undecided project to design, adding that the 'best way to assure this is to have no further publicity' (COP 1–15974). But the *New Republic* published a Lewis Mumford article that scorned the Century of Progress for excluding Wright, comparing his treatment with that of Louis Sullivan at the World's Columbian Exposition. Lewis Mumford, 'A tale of two fairs,' *New Republic*, LXV, 21 January 1931, pp. 271–72.

5   D. H. Burnham diary, 23 May 1928, BBC; Nathaniel Owings, *The Spaces in Between: An Architect's Journey*, Boston, 1973, p. 46; Harvey Wiley Corbett to Rufus Dawes, 25 May 1928, COP 5–41; John Holabird to Hubert Burnham, 21 January 1930, COP 5–29.

6   Corbett to Dawes, 25 May 1928; Memorandum on fees paid to Architectural Commission, 16 June 1933, COP 5–42a.

7   Trustees' Meeting, 7 December 1928, COP 3–40; Minutes of second Architectural Commission meeting, 5–7 December 1928, COP 5–41; Allen D. Albert, Report on permanent buildings at world's fairs, n.d., COP 5–543a.

8   Minutes of second Architectural Commission meeting, 5–7 December 1928, COP 5–41.

9   Minutes of third Architectural Commission meeting, 21–23 January 1929, COP 5–41.

10 Memorandum of informal meeting, 26 September 1929, COP 5–40; Minutes of sixth Architectural Commission meeting, 28–30 October 1929, COP 5–40; Minutes of seventh Architectural Commission meeting, 19–21 December 1929, COP 5–39; D. H. Burnham diary, 29 October 1929, BBC.

11 Minutes of sixth Architectural Commission meeting, 28–30 October 1929, COP 5–40. See also the undated memo concerning the procedures designed to facilitate 'understanding and contact' between the Architectural Commission and the Board of Trustees, COP 5–29.

12 *Chicago Tribune*, 16 February 1930; Rufus Dawes to Lenox Lohr, 27 February 1930, COP 9–33.

13 Minutes of the eighth Architectural Commission meeting, 17–19 March 1930, COP 5–39.

14 Minutes of the ninth Architectural Commission meeting, 19–21 May 1930, COP 5–39.

15 Allen D. Albert to Harvey Wiley Corbett, 10 April 1930, COP 5–18b; Carl Lindefeld to Louis Skidmore, 5 September 1930, COP 5–24; *Chicago Tribune*, 15 July 1931; Clarence W. Farrier to Raymond Hood, 21 July 1931, COP 5–23; Hood to Farrier, 22 October 1931, COP 5–23; Daniel Burnham to Hood, 24 May 1932, COP 5–22; Hood to Burnham, 22 June 1932, COP 5–22; Burnham to Hood, 24 June 1932; Lenox R. Lohr, *Fair Management: The Story of a Century of Progress Exposition*, Chicago, 1952, p. 98.

16   Cathy Cahan and Richard Cahan, 'The lost city of the depression,' *Chicago History*, IV, Winter 1976–77, p. 237; Ralph Walker, Report on tower of water and light, 4 March 1932, COP 5–36; Ralph Walker, Report on tower of steel, n.d., COP 5–36. John Stephen Sewell, the director of exhibits, favored a proposition sent by a Mr Grant for a 1,600 to 2,000-foot steel tower, which would remain 'for many years as the outstanding beacon of the world.' Sewell to Lenox Lohr, 21 March 1931, COP 11–13.

17   Owings, *Spaces*, pp. 47–48, 51–53; A. N. Gonsior, 'Report of the special features division,' pp. 67–72, COP 15–102; Minutes of Architectural Commission meeting, 11–13 April 1932, COP 5–37.

18   Memorandum, Architectural Commission, 30 December 1931, COP 5–42a.

19   Clarence W. Farrier and Bert M. Thorud, 'Design of the world's fair buildings,' *Western Society of Engineers*, XXXV, October 1930, pp. 384–86; Clarence W. Farrier, 'Exposition buildings unique in form and structure,' *Engineering News-Record*, CX, 2 March 1933, pp. 278–82.

20   Raymond Willoughby, 'Building tells the story of progress,' *Nation's Business*, XXI, June 1933, pp. 22–24; Daniel H. Burnham, 'Skyscrapers of the future,' *Popular Mechanics*, LVIII, August 1932, pp. 177–79, 118A, 120A.

21   George W. Gray, 'Bizarre patterns for the Chicago fair,' *New York Times Sunday Magazine*, 6 March 1932; 'The Chicago world's fair: a Century of Progress,' *Commercial Art and Industry* [London], XIV, March 1933, pp. 99–100.

22   Among books detailing the evolution of architecture and design during this period are Bevis Hillier, *The Style of the Century, 1900–1980*, London, 1983; Martin Greif, *Depression Moderne: The Thirties Style in America*, New York, 1975; Eva Weber, *Art Deco in America*, New York, 1985; and Jeffrey Meikle, *Twentieth Century Limited: Industrial Design in America, 1925–1939*, Philadelphia, 1979.

23   Ada Louise Huxtable, 'You can't go home to these fairs again,' *New York Times*, 28 October 1973; *Chicago Tribune*, 12 March 1989.

24   Louis Skidmore, 'The Hall of Science, a Century of Progress Exposition: details of structure and equipment,' *Architectural Forum*, LVII, October 1932, pp. 361–66; Farrier and Thorud, 'Design of the world's fair buildings,' pp. 386–87.

25   Clarence W. Farrier, 'The gadgets: shelters, flags, decoration,' *Architectural Record*, LXXIII, May 1933, pp. 363–65.

26   'Forum of Events,' *Architectural Record*, LXXIV, December 1933, p. 27. For a similar appraisal, see Almus Pratt Evans, 'Exposition architecture: 1893 versus 1933,' *Parnassus*, V, May 1933, pp. 17–21. According to Evans, the dignified architecture of the World's Columbian Exposition suited the 'imperial spirit' of the times, while at the Century of Progress, order had given way to 'a mad panorama of frenzied temples, strung in sensational array.'

27   A. M. Frankfurter, 'Architecture of a Century of Progress,' *Fine Arts*, XX, July 1933, pp. 5–11; 'Thumb tacks and T-square,' *Architect and Engineer*, CXV, October 1933, p. 4.

28   Eugene Klaber, 'World's fair architecture,' *American Magazine of Art*, XXVI, January 1933, pp. 293–98.

29   *Ibid.*, p. 298.

30   'Chrysler exhibition building,' *Architectural Forum*, LIX, December 1933, pp. 455–58; Arthur F. Woltersdorf, 'Carnival architecture,' *American Architect*, CXLIII, July 1933, p. 20. R. L. Duffus, writing in the *New York Times Sunday Magazine*,

concluded that 'if the people of the United States are not pylon-conscious before November 1, it will not be the fault of the Century of Progress.' See his article, 'The fair: a world of tomorrow,' *New York Times Sunday Magazine*, 28 May 1933.

Many years later, Carl Condit, in an essay written during the early planning for the proposed 1992 Chicago world's fair, noted that the three most important architectural legacies from the Century of Progress were the use of vivid color, which did not survive the adoption of the International Style by American architects, the suspended roof of the Travel and Transport Building, and the multivault concrete shell roof built in 1934 for the Brook Hill Farm Dairy exhibit. These techniques, known in Europe but new to the United States, were incorporated into American building over time. See Carl Condit, 'The Century of Progress exposition: an outline of its contributions to the building arts,' 1992 World's Fair Forum Papers, Northwestern University, Evanston, Ill., April 1984.

6   Bright colors and neon lights

> The splendid symphonic crash of colors suggests the great moment in Wagner's Rheingold when Thor strikes the rock from which leaps the rainbow bridge spanning the Rhine.[1]

Perhaps the strongest impression most visitors carried away from the Century of Progress was the rainbow of colors seen on the fair buildings and all the various decorative items splashed around the fairgrounds. The problem of color became a major consideration for the Architectural Commission in early 1931, when the depression was forcing the architects to look for alternative ways to decorate their buildings and when the paint that had been applied to the Administration Building in the fall of 1930 proved to be an esthetic disaster because of a chemical disagreement between the paint and the exterior asbestos board. In February 1931, the commission agreed that a color specialist should be appointed, but it was not until January 1932 that it called on Joseph Urban to draw up an overall color scheme for the fair. In April, Urban's responsibility was enlarged to co-ordinate light and landscaping with color.[2]

Urban, a well-known designer of Broadway stage sets, had first been engaged by the Century of Progress in May 1930 to do some color studies of the Administration and Travel and Transport Buildings. With the growing importance of color to the exposition, however, the commission made Urban a fellow member in 1932 and paid him $25,000 ($10,000 in gold notes) on the condition that he would be on the site for the four months prior to the opening of the fair.[3]

There were really two problems involved: the colors to be used and their relationship to one another, and the types of paint to be used, taking into consideration the vicissitudes of the weather and the variety of surfaces to be painted. While Urban devised the color scheme, it was his associate Otto Teegen who took charge of the application of paint to exterior surfaces and who had to deal with the problem of paint types. In charge of interior color was Shepard Vogelgesang, who became director of color for the 1934 season following Urban's death on 10 July 1933.

The use of color on buildings had no tradition in the history of world's fairs. The World's Columbian Exposition had, of course, been widely known and praised as the White City, and the dazzling whiteness of the classically styled buildings around the Court of Honor had been one of the strongest images of that fair. Pastel colors had been used at the Pan-American Exposition in Buffalo in 1901 and the Panama-Pacific International Exposition in San Francisco in 1915, but in neither case was color a dominant decorative feature. Some of the European fairs of the late 1920s and early 1930s had utilized color to a greater degree than ever before, and D. H. Burnham, Jr., had been so impressed with the colorfulness of the 1931 Paris Colonial Exposition that he recommended adjusting the budget to allow for more color at the Century of Progress. It is not clear how much weight Burnham's recommendation carried, but never before had a fair featured the bold, dramatic, intense colors that made up Joseph Urban's palette for the Century of Progress.

Urban's color scheme consisted of twenty-three intensely bright colors. These included white, gray, black, aluminum, and gold, as well as six shades of orange and yellow, three shades of red, and nine shades of blue and green. Urban called for the use of three or four colors on most buildings, and he specified that 20 per cent of the painted surfaces should be white, 20 per cent blue, 20 per cent orange, 15 per cent black, and the remaining 25 per cent divided among the other colors. He wanted the colors used in ways that would emphasize the architectural characteristics of each building, while at the same time co-ordinating larger groups of buildings. In addition, the bright colors were also important in creating a carnival spirit for the fair. Generally speaking, the architectural commission favored Urban's color plan, although Arthur Brown questioned the number of strong colors, and Paul Philippe Cret wondered how such colors would hold up under varied weather conditions. Edward Bennett, on the other hand, questioned the politics of using the color red: 'The wholesale use of red such as proposed in the Government area cannot, I believe, escape the criticism of association with ideas of government not acceptable in this country.'[4]

Weather conditions were just one of Otto Teegen's problems. Not only did he have to find a paint that would stand up under weather that ranged from the cold rainy days of a late spring or early fall in Chicago to the bright sunny days of July and August, he also had to find paint that would adhere for at least eight months to a wide variety of surfaces. And, of course, the paint had to take color pigments sufficient to satisfy Urban's scheme and also look as attractive under artificial illumination as in natural daylight. Finally, he had to arrange to have 15,000 gallons of paint applied in just thirty-three working days, since inclement weather made it impossible to do any significant exterior painting before the end of March.

Most of the Century of Progress buildings were sheathed in $\frac{1}{2}$-inch gypsum board that had been primed with aluminum paint. Some buildings, particularly those with curved surfaces, had sheet metal siding, while others utilized plywood, asbestos cement board or Masonite. The Sky-Ride was built of structural steel, and footbridges were wood. Building foundations were concrete, stucco was used on parts of the Electrical Group, and here and there one could find exposed plaster or galvanized steel in need of paint.

The American Asphalt Paint Company provided the three types of paint that were tested. Aluminum-based paint was tried because the small bits of aluminum in the paint would, it was hoped, counteract the alkalinity of certain kinds of wall surfaces. Oil-based paint was the most common form of paint available, but Teegen and his staff found that casein paint, which was water-based, worked best on the widest variety of surfaces.

Union considerations were also significant. The painter's union allowed their members to use only a $4\frac{1}{2}$-inch brush with oil-based paint, but if casein paint were used, they could use either a 10-inch brush or mechanical spraying devices. In general, the painters worked with the 10-inch brushes, since most did not know how to spray paint, and those who did found the wind off the lake to be an obstacle too great to overcome.[5]

Urban and Teegen worked out a color geography, or orientation, that helped guide the decision as to which colors to apply to which surfaces. For the most part, cool colors (blues, greens, violets) were used on the north sides of buildings, while neutral colors (white, gray, gold, aluminum, black) were used on the east and west sides, and warm colors (reds, oranges, yellows) were used on the south sides. This was done in part because of the way the colors would look under sunlight and partly out of concern for permanence; cool colors stand up least well under bright sunlight.

In general, the façades of buildings followed the geographical formula, although recessed areas on the south sides of buildings were painted with cool colors if there was reasonable protection from the sun. For example, the north side of the Hall of Science was gray violet and gray-blue, with accents of gold and red. The south side was red, orange, and yellow, with some white and gray, and dark blue accents in shaded places. The east and west sides were mostly gray and white, with orange and yellow accents. The foundations of the Hall of Science and all other buildings were painted a uniform gray-green to provide a neutral background for landscaping.

Color was also used to show off unusual architectural features of fair buildings. Nowhere was this better seen than on the Travel and Transport Building. On this building, which faced east, decorative elements, such as the fins setting off the entrance, were red, the many exposed structural members were black, shadowed areas were blue, and most of the rest was gray, with aluminum and white accents. The distinctive suspended roof of the building was painted aluminum.

Night effects were also a consideration. Shining colored light on neutral surfaces, or white light on colored surfaces, tends to bleach out the color and produce an unsatisfactory effect. But shining colored light on colored surfaces can be effective without an extravagant use of power, if one is careful in selecting what kind of light to use with surfaces of different colors.[6]

As Felix Payant, the editor of *Design* wrote, the Century of Progress was the 'largest stage set [Urban] ever did.' And while Payant felt that Urban had succeeded in bringing the architectural elements together with his colors, other critics were not so favorably impressed. Arthur Woltersdorf concluded that the color scheme contributed to the disintegration of the design rather than to its unity. The blacks, reds, and blues of the Electrical Group, he wrote, appeared 'almost barbaric,' while the predominant whiteness of the Hall of Science was 'insipid.' Perhaps Douglas Haskell, the critic for *Architectural Review*, was only being coy when he wrote that sunglasses were sold at the entrance gates 'to protect [the] eyes against the sun and the buildings.' Only by wearing colored glasses, said Haskell, could the visitor see a unified design in the face of the intense colors; Urban's colors 'pulled apart the individual buildings, if they hadn't already been by jagged angles and shapes.' The only truly restful building, one that did not fall under Urban's responsibility, was the Sweden pavilion, in tan stucco with gray trim and blue accenting around the entrance.

Even Nathaniel Owings, who was part of the fair management and who by his own account had a great experience in Chicago, seemed a bit less than exuberant when he wrote that the large, flat, windowless wall surfaces created an eerie sense when painted in 'crude, primitive, startling' color combinations. Still, Payant was probably correct when he concluded that while future buildings may not use the intense colors of the Century of Progress, builders would have to take color more into account in their planning.[7]

Together with color, artificial lighting was a major decorative component of the Century of Progress. As early as the Southern Exposition in Louisville, Kentucky, in 1883, the wonders of electric lighting had thrilled fairgoers with night-time vistas. Lighting had been an important feature of the World's Columbian Exposition, with the major buildings outlined with strings of incandescent lights. All the fairs after 1893 had included a pavilion devoted to electricity, and the Palais de Electricité at the Paris world's fair of 1900 was arguably the most spectacular building there. The Tower of Jewels, the signature structure at the 1915 Panama-Pacific International Exposition in San Francisco, achieved its jewel-like effect by means of lights shining through bits of colored glass attached to the tower. By 1915 also, floodlighting was practicable, and special effects were produced by reflecting bright lights off the walls of buildings, although the buildings had to be white or pastel-colored for the desired effect to be achieved.

In 1929, Daniel H. Burnham had gone to Spain to visit the Barcelona and Seville expositions, and he had been particularly impressed by the night-time illumination at Barcelona, which 'far surpasses all previous expositions . . . [and] was what we have dreamed of for Chicago in 1933.' The buildings and fountains simultaneously changed colors, like the electric fountains of earlier fairs. The main axis had large glass towers that also changed colors, and on all the terraces, there were 'lotus-like glass fountains that shimmered in the long delicate tendrils like water jets in a fountain.'[8]

Technological advances in lighting had come a long way between 1915 and 1933, and Century of Progress managers early on made the decision to place considerable emphasis on lighting for dramatic and decorative effects. Incandescent lighting had become brighter and more highly concentrated, color screens or filters of various materials were available to flood wall surfaces with colored light, and gaseous tube lighting, utilizing inert gases such as neon, could produce brilliant colours of lights in glass tubes that could be formed into any desired shape.

At a meeting of the Architectural Commission in December 1929, Lenox

Chicago's great world's fairs

Lohr reported on a trip that he had made to New York to see Owen D. Young and D'Arcy Ryan of General Electric (GE), who offered the use of GE's laboratories and materials for research and testing lighting systems. The noted industrial designer Norman Bel Geddes was approved as illumination consultant, and Ryan, who was the director of GE's illuminating engineering laboratory, was appointed advisor on lighting. In 1931, the Architectural Commission urged Lohr to attend the Paris Colonial Exposition to see what he could learn about the lighting effects there.[9]

As D'Arcy Ryan expressed it, the function of Century of Progress lighting was to help bring together groups of buildings into a more 'unified whole.' Lighting could also be used to create the impression of greater height, or to present a more 'dignified and restful' effect. The unusual architecture and color of the Century of Progress made new demands on lighting engineers; moreover, consideration of fog, smoke, and a limited budget all had to be taken into account.

In late 1932, General Electric's principal competitor, Westinghouse, was brought in to help with the lighting, and in February 1933, the board of trustees formally contracted with both companies for the development and installation of 'exterior lighting and illumination' for a minimum of $350,000, payable in gold notes. Under the guidance of Ryan, the two electric giants supplied the fair with more than 15,000 incandescent lamps, 24 36-inch arc searchlights, 1,000 1,000-watt floodlights, 2,200 200-watt floodlights, 17 3-kilowatt searchlights, and 500 45-inch high mushroom light fixtures, as well as special lighting effects for the fountains in the lagoons. The architecture of the fair dictated specially designed lighting fixtures, but despite the fears of some, light efficiency was not noticeably impaired, and some critics thought they worked better as practical lighting fixtures rather than as decorative elements.[10]

This was the first fair at which gaseous tube lighting was seen, and it was used in many different locations. Normally, visitors did not see the tubes themselves, but only the colored light reflected from building surfaces. One exception was at the rear of the court of the Electrical Group, where 4,650 feet of green and blue tube lighting was arranged so as to create the effect of a 55-foot high 'cascade,' over the objections of Raymond Hood, the architect, who had argued for a real waterfall. One standard exterior lighting fixture, seen at different places on the site, utilized a series of alternating mercury and neon gaseous tubes. The variously colored light was seen through louvres cut into 38-foot high triangular standards. Although neon tube lighting had been introduced into the United

States in 1923, the Century of Progress and later fairs in the 1930s contributed much to the popularization of this form of lighting, particularly in signage and on movie theaters.[11]

For its own corporate exhibit in the Electrical Group, Westinghouse created one of the most spectacular lighting effects of the fair. This was erected on a series of eight 70-foot high towers situated behind a 12-foot balcony prominently displaying the word 'Westinghouse.' On each tower were eleven illuminated disks, 10 inches in diameter, 8 inches thick, and 4 feet apart, lit by red, white, blue, and amber lights in varying combinations. This produced 'a panorama of rainbow colors never before created in a lighting display . . . [that] will be remembered with the vividness of a reddened sun in a beautiful sunset.'[12]

Searchlights were used to set the fairgrounds apart from the lights of nearby downtown Chicago. At the southern end of the site, there was a bank of twenty-four 36-inch arc searchlights that fanned the beams out over the fair, often crossing with the beams of another bank of seventeen 36-inch incandescent searchlights located near the Electrical Group. Other distinctive lighting was seen in the fountains. There were three in the south lagoon and one in the court of the Electrical Group. Each of the lagoon fountains had 507 water jets, nozzles and sprays, and each had eight programmed displays lasting seventy-five seconds, with water lit by colored lights and pumped up as high as 80 feet. Occasionally, smoke bombs were utilized to add to the dramatic impact of the light show.[13]

Westinghouse devised the special sidewalk lighting used at the Century of Progress. As spokesman L. A. S. Wood told *the Literary Digest*, 'A new method of illuminating the exposition grounds will be used. As a result, while the grounds will be well lighted with white light, the visitor will find himself walking about in a shallow sea of light containing all the colors of the rainbow.' This was accomplished through a new kind of fixture, called 'mushroom luminaries,' consisting of an aluminum base and an inverted cone of a colored translucent material called 'micarta.' Inside the cone was a set of refracting prisms and an electric bulb. The prisms were adjusted so that white light from the bulb was directed down to the sidewalk, while colored light was directed up through the translucent walls of the cone to produce a low intensity but glowing colored light.[14]

Because the fair buildings contained practically no windows, a decision occasioned by economic considerations and the desire to have consistent lighting for the exhibits at all times of the day and in all kinds of weather, interior lighting was an important consideration. For the most part, ceiling or indirect cove lighting was used in the exhibit areas, and indirect lighting, at 75 per cent of the exhibit area intensity, was installed behind signage in the corridors. Special lighting was designed for large exhibit halls and for showcases.[15]

The lighting for the Century of Progress was successful in achieving its main objective – to make the fair look different at night than it did in the day. Douglas Haskell, the *Architecture Review* critic, summed up the feelings of most observers when he wrote that the many varieties of light made the fair lovely at night. He thought that the floodlighting was effective in softening the angularity of the buildings and that neon had been employed to especially good effect.[16]

Ever since the advent of electric lighting, fairs have frequently had a more dramatic look at night. The comparatively primitive electric lighting at the World's Columbian Exposition, where each of the main buildings was outlined by strings of lights, still appeared as one of the visual marvels of that fair. And most critics thought that the night-time vistas of the Century of Progress, when the lighting effects softened the brilliance of the strong colors, gave visitors to that fair a very special memory.

Notes

1　F. Crissey, 'Why the Century of Progress architecture?,' *Saturday Evening Post*, CCV, 10 June 1933, p. 64.

2　Minutes of meeting with Chicago architects, 13 February 1–31, COP 5–38; Minutes of ninth Architectural Commission meeting, 19–21 May 1930, COP 5–39; Minutes of Architectural Commission meeting, 11–13 April 1932, COP 5–37.

3　Minutes of Architectural Commission meeting, 11–13 April 1932, COP 5–37.

4　Minutes of Architectural Commission meeting, 11–13 April 1932, COP 5–37. Unsigned letter from Shepard Vogelgesang to Edward H. Bennett, 28 March 1934, COP 5–10; 'Business and "the fair",' *Business Week*, 31 May 1933, pp. 12–13; *Chicago Tribune*, 11 July 1933.

5　Otto Teegen, 'Painting the exposition buildings,' *Architectural Record*, LXXIII, May 1933, pp. 366–68.

6　'Century of Progress exposition,' *The Painters Magazine*, LIX, June 1932, pp. 9–10; Teegen, 'Painting,' p. 366.

7　Felix Payant, 'The editor's page,' *Design*, XXXV, October 1933, p. 1; Arthur F. Woltersdorf, 'Carnival architecture,' *American Architect*, CXLIII, July 1933, p. 13; Douglas Haskell, 'Mixed metaphors at Chicago,' *Architectural Review*, LXXIV, August 1933, pp. 47–48; Nathaniel Owings, *The Spaces in Between: An Architect's Journey*, Boston, 1973, pp. 56–57.

8　Daniel H. Burnham diary, 23–24 September 1929, BBC.

9　Minutes of seventh Architectural Commission meeting, 19–20 December 1929, COP

5–39; Minutes of Architectural Commission meeting, 29 September–1 October 1931, COP 5–38; Farrier, 'Exposition buildings,' p. 282.

10   Meeting of COP executive committee, 9 February 1933, COP 3–19; 'Weird lights at Chicago fair,' *Literary Digest*, CXV, 25 March 1933, p. 32; George A. Barclay, 'Modern architecture dominates Century of Progress exposition,' *Architect and Engineer*, CXIII, June 1933, pp. 21, 24; W. D'Arcy Ryan, 'Lighting a Century of Progress,' *Electrical Engineering*, LIII, May 1934, pp. 732–34.

11   Rudi Stern, *The New Let There Be Neon*, New York, 1988, pp. 19–24, 27; Ryan, 'Lighting,' p. 734.

12   'Aurora Borealis in the Westinghouse Century of Progress exhibit,' *Display World*, XII, May 1933, p. 25.

13   Ryan, 'Lighting,' p. 736; J. L. McConnell, 'Lighting heads the list of special facilities,' *Engineering News-Record*, CX, 2 March 1933, p. 284. See also H. W. Magee, 'Building with light,' *Popular Mechanics*, LVIII, July 1932, pp. 8–14.

14   'Weird lights,' p. 32.

15   McConnell, 'Lighting heads the list,' p. 283.

16   Haskell, 'Mixed metaphors,' pp. 48–49.

7   Science: the key to progress

Science Finds – Industry Applies – Man Conforms.[1]

When the idea of celebrating the centennial of the founding of Chicago with a world's fair was first broached in the mid-1920s, most of those involved spoke of such a fair in terms of showing off the progress of Chicago since the World's Columbian Exposition in 1893 and in what benefits a 1933 fair could bring to the city. Rufus Dawes knew, however, that a successful fair would have to have a broader theme than one limited to the past, present, and future of the host city.

In the fall of 1927, Dawes met with George E. Hale, an astrophysicist and the director of the Mt Wilson Observatory, who urged Dawes to have the fair focus on the 'services of science to humanity,' since the one hundred years of Chicago's existence corresponded nicely with the era of the greatest advances in pure science as well as the industrial revolution in the United States, the product of applied science. When he met with Mayor Thompson and other civic leaders in December 1927 to muster their support for holding an exposition in Chicago, Dawes only alluded vaguely to the theme of scientific progress, but in January 1928, Dr Michael Pupin, a physicist from Columbia University, spoke with Dawes and the newly formed board of trustees and suggested the National Research Council as the agency to organize the scientific activities of the fair.[2]

The National Research Council (NRC) was a child of the National Academy of Sciences. Born in 1916 out of an offer from the Academy to President Woodrow Wilson to co-ordinate non-governmental scientific and technological resources for effective utilization in the coming war, the NRC became an umbrella organization that set up specialized committees to deal with specific problems. In 1918, Wilson asked that the NRC be perpetuated, since its services might be just as useful in peacetime as in wartime. What the president had in mind was an organization that would promote research in pure and applied sciences to strengthen national defense and contribute to public welfare. The National Academy of Sciences saw this as an opportunity to increase its influence in academic and corporate America and reorganized the NRC in 1919 into a co-operative organization of eighty professional societies representing the various fields of sciences, engineering, and industrial technology.[3]

During the early months of 1928, Dawes continued to have informal discussions with a number of NRC leaders, persuading them that the world's fair needed help in presenting its theme of 'demonstrating the service of science to humanity, especially through industries.' On 21 August 1928, the board of trustees formally requested the 'advice and assistance' of the NRC. The chairman of the council, Dr George K. Burgess, appointed a committee headed by Dr Frank B. Jewett, a vice-president of the American Telephone & Telegraph Company (AT & T), to see how the NRC might best respond to the fair board's request.

Jewett's committee, which included Pupin and Dr William Allen Pusey, a former president of the American Medical Association who was also a member of the fair's board of trustees, reported back to the NRC executive committee in February 1929, urging that the NRC involve itself fully with the exposition by creating a larger, more broadly representative committee. This committee, which became known as the Science Advisory Committee (SAC), consisted of representatives from many of the NRC's constituent organizations as well as several at-large members chosen because of their experience in public affairs or applied science. The functions of this committee were threefold: to determine a 'philosophy' for the Century of Progress, to give advice on relevant matters to exposition managers, and when necessary, to mediate disputes over specific scientific exhibits.[4]

The SAC itself had a membership of 34, but each of these individuals formed a sub-committee, which increased the total number involved to 432. Over a four-month period in late 1929 and early 1930, these sub-committees met and produced reports that did much to shape the philosophy and exhibit plan of the Century of Progress. The philosophy that emerged from these reports was, to use Pupin's term, 'scientific idealism:' the 'deification' of science displayed in a 'Temple of Pure Science,' where 'thoughtful' visitors would receive a 'quiet unconscious schooling,' learning that 'science is at the root of most of the material things and many of the social things which make up modern life.'

In addition, the SAC report included some suggestions relating to possible exhibits. The Temple of Pure Science should be the central feature of the fair, an architecturally striking building that would symbolically represent science. It should contain some 125,000 square feet of exhibit space, the exhibits should show the methods and influence of science and 'strike the dominant note' of the exposition. Applications of sciences should be represented by industrial exhibits in 750,000 square feet of space. The SAC suggested that the earth science exhibits be housed in and around an artificial mountain range, but not one so big as to dwarf other features of the fair. Since a replica of a Maya Temple was already in the planning stage, the committee recommended that its interior be used for anthropological exhibits illustrating the development of human-kind on the American continent.[5]

The Century of Progress board of trustees received the SAC report on 7 May 1930, and forwarded it and the sub-committee reports to North-western University physics professor Dr Henry Crew, who was responsible for planning the basic sciences exhibits. The SAC thought it could be most helpful at this point by surveying sources of exhibit material of the five basic sciences, by co-ordinating the display of that material in the Temple of Science (later rechristened the Hall of Science), and by pro-ducing a pictorial representation of a typical sub-committee report for the benefit of the exhibits staff. These sub-committee reports turned out to be useful to exhibitors in both the pure and the applied sciences as to the nature of their exhibits. Throughout, the reports emphasized that exhibits should focus on the service of science to mankind and should attempt to show the *process* by which modern industrial products were made, rather than simply displaying the finished product, as had been the standard at past expositions. The reports also suggested that emphasis be placed on how people had progressed to a comfortable accommodation with the physical world. In a practical sense, the Century of Progress profited from the fact that the involvement of so many individuals in this process led to many exhibits being donated or loaned by universities and industry.[6]

The SAC also played a constructive role for the Century of Progress through its public relations work. From November 1930 until May 1931, the committee produced thirty fifteen-minute radio broadcasts promoting a bright future for a scientifically-led America. The programs received much fan mail, and copies of the transcripts were sent to universities and engineering schools. In addition, press releases sent out to newspapers and magazines produced an estimated 5,000 columns of educational material.

By the summer of 1931, the Century of Progress was well into its con-struction phase, and the board of trustees and the SAC agreed that the latter could be disbanded, although a number of committee members continued as consultants on an individual basis. The committee itself formally ceased to exist on 30 June 1931. During its roughly two years in existence, it had spent just under $90,000 of Century of Progress funds, mostly for staff salaries and meeting expenses.[7]

Although the philosophy was in place and the SAC no longer existed as such, much more remained to be done in the exhibit area to bring about the realization of the fair's grand theme. The SAC, as part of its work, had developed the following exhibitory objectives: 1) show what the principal sciences are; 2) demonstrate the methods of science; 3) portray outstanding discoveries and phenomena; 4) indicate the interdependence of science, modern life, and industrial development; and 5) show the transition from ignorance and superstition to the acceptance of the scientific method. The SAC suggested that these could best be carried out by arranging exhibits so that they told stories and by using a variety of methods, ranging from models to slides to short films. The committee also encouraged exhibit organizers to combine elements of science whenever possible; biology and zoology might be appropriately presented together, for example. These pointers were passed on to Crew and a team of Chicago-area university professors, each of whom was assigned the responsibility of putting together the exhibits in one of the basic sciences.

The exhibit directors included Capt. F. H. Roberts (Mathematics), Dr G. S. Fulcher (Physics), Dr I. E. Muskat (Chemistry), Dr J. F. W. Pearson (Biology), Dr J. Volney Lewis and Dr Carey Croneis (Geology), and Dr E. J. Carey (Medicine). In addition, the board of trustees had added a new division of scientific publications that would co-ordinate the publication of a series of scientific works aimed at the educated layperson. Most of these individuals took to their tasks eagerly, so that by November 1930, Crew could report that the physics and chemistry exhibits were already fairly well outlined and moving ahead, the publications committee had twenty writers lined up, and only the geology exhibit had nothing yet to report.[8]

In August 1930, the board of trustees decided to try and repeat the success they had enjoyed with the National Research Council by inviting the Social Science Research Council to help create an advisory committee on social sciences for the fair, headed first by Dr Howard W. Odum and later by Dr Fay Cooper-Cole and Helen Bennett. The SAC had a committee on anthropology and psychology, thus providing a link between basic sciences and social sciences, and in April 1930, Cole wrote Lohr that anthropology exhibits had been very popular at earlier fairs. Echoing the SAC report, he said that if the Century of Progress wants to 'tell a scientific story,' it should set aside a twenty-five acre space and construct a display showing groups of people from Eskimos to southwestern Indians. In the center of the space, there should be an exhibit of ancient mound builders; at the far end, reproductions of Maya buildings to represent the height of native American civilization prior to the arrival of Europeans. Cole estimated that such an exhibit would cost $500,000 but would include colorful ceremonies and dances and be very popular. More detailed exhibits, he noted, could be placed inside the Maya building.[9]

The Century of Progress was perhaps the first international exposition to take on the responsibility itself of producing a large number of the exhibits. After the SAC report, the board of trustees decided that it would have to do the pure science exhibits in order to maintain faithfulness to the theme; industry would be contracted to sponsor and install the applied science exhibits. To that end, the board created a Basic Science Division to handle the fair-sponsored exhibits in the pure sciences, and an Applied Science and Industry Division that would work co-operatively with the Basic Science Division but be responsible for obtaining the participation of industry. At first, it was hoped to enlist industrial participation as a group through trade associations, but this idea was soon dropped in favor of letting larger industries or individual corporations prepare their own exhibits and take advantage of the obvious public relations value of participating in the fair. To help organize this effort, the Applied Science and Industry Division was subdivided into six topical groups: 1) Travel and Transport; 2) Electrical; 3) Agriculture; 4) Medical and Chemical; 5) General Exhibits; 6) Home and Industrial Arts. The SAC offered strategies to induce industrial participation and promised technical advice on the exhibits but assured the Century of Progress that its members would not be salespeople for the exposition. But even without the SAC out selling the Century of Progress, the initial response from American industry was good; Dawes reported in July 1930 that he had received pledges of co-operation from the Radio Corporation of America (RCA), AT & T, Western Union, a number of railroads, and the electrical industry.[10]

Although the SAC had finished its official chores, its members kept in close touch with the fair management, and many of them attended the gala dedication of the Hall of Science on 1 June 1933. In September 1931, Jewett commiserated with Dawes over the impact of the depression: 'I am only sorry that Fate has played you such a scurvy trick with regard to the conditions under which you must create the exposition.' When the decision was made in August 1932 to proceed with the Arcturus ceremony – using the light of the star Arcturus, forty light years away, to turn on the lights of the Century of Progress – Crew telegraphed Jewett with the news.

At the dedication of the Hall of Science, Crew spoke of the assistance given the fair by the NRC and introduced Jewett, the keynote speaker, who took as his theme the service science provides to civilization and pointed out how important public understanding of scientific progress was in staving off revolutionary threat and preserving a stable social order.[11]

Robert Rydell, in his article, 'The fan dance of science,' concludes that the single-minded purpose of the Century of Progress organizers, working co-operatively with representatives of the National Research Council was to institutionalize the notion that science and the scientific method were the foundation of the modern American corporation and that only through the unity of science and industry could the depression be ended and American culture move ahead. This theme, writes Rydell, was perpetuated in the later fairs of the 1930s, including the New York World's Fair of 1939–40, where, with the depression largely in the past, fair organizers promoted science as the pathway to a golden future.[12]

Notes

1 Century of Progress, *Official Guide Book of the Fair 1933*, Chicago, 1933, p. 11.
2 Robert Rydell, 'The fan dance of science,' *Isis*, LXXVI, 1985, pp. 525–27; Rufus C. Dawes, *Report of the President of a Century of Progress to the Board of Trustees*, Chicago, 1936, pp. 28–29.
3 National Research Council, 'A history of the National Research Council, 1919–1933,' Reprint and Circular Series 106, Washington D.C., 1933, pp. 7–8.
4 Rydell, 'Fan dance,' pp. 527–28; Dawes, *Report of the President*, pp. 29–33; Report of the Science Advisory Committee to the executive board of the National Research Council, June 1931?, COP 5–252.
5 Preliminary report of the Science Advisory Committee, 8 April 1930, COP 5–253; Rydell, 'Fan dance,' p. 529.
6 Report of the Science Advisory Committee, June 1931?, COP 5–252; Dawes, *Report of the President*, pp. 33–35; Memorandum, John Stephen Sewell to Exhibits Department, 19 June 1931, COP 11–18.
7 Report of the Science Advisory Committee, June 1931?, COP 5–252.
8 Rydell, 'Fan dance,' p. 530; R. P. Shaw to Frank R. Little, 7 May 1930, COP 11–6; Henry Crew to John Stephen Sewell, 12 November 1930, COP 11–11.
9 Fay Cooper-Cole to Lenox Lohr, 30 April 1930, COP 5–254; Lenox R. Lohr, *Fair Management: The Story of a Century of Progress Expositions*, Chicago, 1952, pp. 140, 143.

10 J. Franklin Bell, 'Applied science and industry at "A Century of Progress" exposition,' *Scientific Monthly*, XXXVI, March 1933, pp. 281–83; Holland to J. Parker Van Zandt, 25 March 1931, COP 5–251.
11 Frank B. Jewett to Rufus Dawes, 4 September 1931, COP 5–252; Henry Crew to Frank B. Jewett (telegram), 8 August 1932, COP 5–253; Rydell, 'Fan dance,' p. 532.
12 Rydell, 'Fan dance,' p. 535.

8   Process, not product

Of course, this is not like the old fair. I tell you that White City was the most
beautiful thing you ever saw in your life. But this is different. This is a college
education.[1]

The exhibits seen at the Century of Progress were meant to be educational, to carry out the theme of showing the progress of science and technology during the past century. Fair leaders worked hard to assure that
exhibits adhered to the major theme, and that, insofar as possible, exhibits
showed the *process*, not the *product* of science and industry. Much of
the credit for the exhibit phase of the Century of Progress goes to John
Stephen Sewell, an Alabama marble manufacturer who served as director
of exhibits from 1930 until failing health forced his resignation in late
1932, and to Louis Skidmore, who became assistant director of exhibits,
in charge of design, when a design section was set up in 1932. Sewell did
much of the conceptualization of how the exhibits should be presented,
while Skidmore made certain that the exhibits conformed to the design
standards established by the fair management.[2]

In a March 1931 memorandum to Lenox Lohr, Sewell noted the points
wherein the Century of Progress differed from other fairs in the area of
exhibits. First, the Century of Progress itself had undertaken the presentation of a large number of exhibits – those in the basic sciences – and
was using a new method of exhibition; that is, showing visitors how basic
science connects with their daily lives. Applied science exhibits, provided
by business concerns, governments, or other organizations, would be presented from the same point of view. Second, the Century of Progress was
the first world's fair to sell large quantities of exhibit space. This required
a special sales force, and the depression made the selling job difficult, but
the financial success of the fair was largely dependent on these sales.
Third, the Century of Progress was the first fair in which a concerted
effort was made to have each exhibitor's display complete but not be

duplicative of another exhibitor's display, something that would necessitate extensive consultation and compromise among exhibitors. To help with the preparation of these scientific and technological exhibits, the fair board, in June 1932, contracted with the Museum of Science and Industry for the advice and technical assistance of its staff. In return, the museum would receive 25 per cent of any surplus funds from the exposition.[3]

Sewell constantly reiterated to his sales force the emphasis on science (or applications of science) as the basis for Century of Progress exhibits. Although the fair management is preparing the basic sciences exhibits itself, he would say, industry will 'complete the story' with their exhibits. The products of industry are well known, but the 'story back of their creation' is not. If the process is brought out with 'dramatic showmanship,' the public will remember the name of the company. This was important, because the exposition managers wanted businesses to derive every possible benefit from participating in the fair, especially during a depression, but at the same time, businesses had to be convinced that the best way to achieve these benefits was to follow Century of Progress guidelines in their exhibits.

In some cases, however, exhibit ideas were developed by individuals on the exposition staff. These were then taken to the most likely sponsors, who were invited to present them, and generally, the invitations were regarded as compliments by those who were approached and were therefore accepted.

These guidelines were drawn up and enforced by Skidmore and his staff. His design section was there to help exhibitors design their presentations in accordance with the theme of the exposition. All exhibitors using space in the principal theme pavilions, such as the Electrical Group or the General Exhibits Building, were required to submit their final plans and color studies to Skidmore's section in order to avoid duplicated exhibits and to co-ordinate with related exhibitors. Exhibitors were expected to concentrate on creating an effective display within their own space. They were to avoid disruptive elements, such as flashing or brightly colored lights that would attract too much attention to any one exhibit. Similarly, they were to avoid anachronistic elements that clashed either with the exhibit or the design of the exhibit space. Thus, velvet curtains, baroque woodwork, or excessive ornamental detail were forbidden. Finally, exhibitors who produced an exhibit involving motion for no other purpose than attracting attention were told to make the motion produce something or get rid of it.[4]

Raymond Hood, a member of the Architectural Commission, suggested that exhibits reflect the 'more human and fundamental interests' of people. The proper place to display an electric ice box, he wrote, is in a home setting, not next to a locomotive or a generator. Only in this way would the ice box be properly appreciated by a 'woman who must be preoccupied with the thoughts of shelter, or the home.'[5]

Questions of how much space should be allotted to various industries and how charges should be made were frequently discussed in the planning stages of the fair. At a meeting held in August 1930, a number of conclusions concerning the specifics of exhibits was reached. There would be no special building erected for the achievements of women or of any race or ethnic group. Space for particular industries would be allocated either on the degree of interest the public has in a particular industry, or on what that industry was willing to do. There would be no charge for space utilized by a collective industrial exhibit, except for a share of advertising expenses.

In November 1930, Sewell advised C. W. Fitch, one of Lohr's assistant managers, that greater efforts should be made to attract exhibits from industries whose products were derived from specific scientific inventions and were considered to be of great importance to the general public. For example, these would include the electrical and transportation industries, along with communications devices like the telegraph, telephone, and radio. On the other hand, the interior marble industry (Sewell's own line of work) was affected by science in ways that were not readily apparent to the public, nor were there revolutionary inventions involved; thus, such an industry need not exhibit.[6]

As mentioned earlier, the basic science exhibits were concentrated in the Hall of Science, although some closely related technological exhibits were in the Electrical Group, which included the Electrical Building, Radio Hall, Communication Hall, and the Edison Memorial. In the Hall of Science were exhibits pertaining to mathematics, physics, chemistry, geology, biology, and medicine. For the most part, these exhibits strove to tell a story in layperson's terms and to include some kind of dynamic element to pique the visitor's interest.

In the mathematics section, the goal was to give a comprehensive view of the subject rather than teach a mathematics course. Thus the exhibit was subdivided into four parts; namely, numbers and algebra, geometry, analysis, and applied mathematics. The center of the exhibit was a large octagonal prism with screens on three sides on which rear-projected slides told the history of the four math areas noted above. The geometry exhibit included a 'spectacular' display of Pollock's methods, with changing combinations of light and string surfaces that highlighted various geometric shapes, all in a 'setting of dignified beauty.' The applied mathematics area contained gyroscopes and other naval instruments to show the relation between mathematics and navigation and an exhibit explaining the mathematical principles behind the law of supply and demand in the field of economics.

In physics, the objective was to create a greater interest in and appreciation of the beauty of nature's workings. There were ninety exhibits in all, arranged in order of an 'ascending frequency scale,' beginning with molecular physics and sound and progressing through to cosmic rays. These were all related to one another by means of a large chart at one end of the hall showing all wave frequencies in relation to one another and to man. Specific exhibits attempted to answer practical questions such as how air holds up an automobile tire and why water drops are round. A display on sound explained how sounds are made and how it is reproduced on film.

The chemistry exhibit was keynoted by a giant periodic table of the elements, which some considered the 'central feature of the entire Exposition.' The display was 30 feet by 25 feet, included a small sample of each element, and was topped by a 10-foot revolving globe that indicated where the principal sources of the more common elements were located. Other exhibits included a diorama of a working sulfur mine, a display of Brownian movement in colloid chemistry, a miniature oil refinery, and a presentation on the processing of rubber from a milky latex to the finished product. Food chemistry was highlighted by a 10-foot tall robot who gave a twenty minute lecture and demonstration on food constituents and how the body digests them.

The geology presentation focused on the origins and growth of the earth and featured active displays of earthquakes, spouting geysers, and erupting volcanoes. Visitors could use model seismographs to measure the intensity of miniature earthquakes produced by small charges of dynamite.

In the biology area, visitors could see a highly magnified twig mechanically simulated to add a year's growth in little more than a minute and highly magnified water that showed visitors the micro-organisms living in it. Other exhibits told the story of evolution from a simple cell to modern humankind.

No other similar world's fair had ever developed a medical exhibit.

Planned by Dr William Allen Pusey, a member of the fair board, the exhibit was built around the Transparent Man, a life-size model with all the organs visible and illuminated. In addition, there were exhibits showing the growth of a human embryo, the development of modern surgery, and diseases of the digestive tract.[7]

While the science exhibits were carefully prepared and certainly more lively than anything similar at previous expositions, there was still a great deal of information for visitors to absorb. Bruce Bliven, whose cynical account of the Century of Progress stands apart from most other reviews, doubted that people seeing these exhibits would learn anything, since there was so much that it all 'melt[s] in [one's] mind into a few vague, confused impressions of machines working.'[8]

Applied science or industrial exhibit space was sold for $10 a square foot, and by opening day there were 511 exhibitors, including 32 that had built their own pavilions. Unlike earlier fairs, where exhibits had customarily competed for prizes, the fair board decided to have no competitive exhibits in order not to detract from the theme of science serving progress. For the 1933 season, a total of $3,742,865 was obtained from the sale of exhibit space, mostly to business or industry, although some space was sold to states and to non-profit organizations.[9]

As indicated earlier, the emphasis in exhibiting was on process rather than product, and this led to some spectacular exhibits by a number of large corporations. The $1.6 million General Motors Building, the largest structure provided by a private business concern, contained an entire Chevrolet assembly line. Not to be outdone, the Chrysler exhibit covered seven acres, with a one-quarter mile oval testing track, on which visitors could ride in cars driven by famous movie stunt men or race car drivers. Firestone's pavilion contained a complete tire factory, fronted by a 'singing color fountain,' while the Nash Motor Company, whose original plan for a pavilion in the shape of a 60-foot high Nash had been rejected, constructed an open elevator for automobiles, so that visitors could see the latest models of Nashes slowly going up and down. Other corporations, perhaps harder hit by the depression, had more modest presentations. General Electric attracted visitors with auto and airplane ride simulators, while Standard Oil Company of Indiana, which occupied the entire second floor of the Travel and Transport Building, showed films about the petroleum industry.[10]

More typical, perhaps, was the tin can exhibit in the General Exhibits Building, a collective presentation of that industry. The exhibit attracted a million visitors in 1934 because it was a 'machine in motion.' A chrome-plated machine, known as The Princess, churned out souvenir banks in the shape of cans for twelve hours a day each of the 159 days of the fair without ever breaking down. Visitors who were willing to wait in line were rewarded with one of these banks which had a colorful picture of the world's fair skyline lithographed on them. As a backdrop to the exhibit, there was an extensive display of canned goods, so many that one visitor was heard to say, 'They must have everything here that's made of tin – except Ford bodies!'[11]

Typical of an agricultural exhibit, perhaps, was the dairy exhibit. The dairy industry was the only food industry to have its own pavilion, and its exhibit was a fairly straightforward sales pitch based on the premise that milk is good for one's health and there is no substitute for dairy products. If people consumed more dairy products, it would 'help them get the things out of life they want most.' The pavilion, a 'colorful, rotund' building that cost $210,000, contained an Industry Hall, a Commodity Hall, an auditorium, a clubroom, a library, and, of course, a dairy café, but the centerpiece of the exhibit was a 'cycloramic wall,' two stories high by 80 feet long. By the projection of light, color, and silhouettes, accompanied by narration and organ music, the 'romantic story of the dairy cow and her products' was told in a five or six minute program. Cows were also part of the exhibit in the International Harvester hall, located in the Agricultural Building. A mechanical cow that 'does everything a human (sic) cow can do' was the main attraction, but one rural visitor was unimpressed: 'She don't do anything my cow don't do.'[12]

If milk was good for the body, then religion was good for the soul, and to make that point, George W. Dixon, chairman of the Committee on Religion for the Century of Progress, organized a $100,000 exhibit in the Hall of Religion, located south of the Hall of Science near the General Exhibits Building. In contrast to the comparative and intellectual nature of the World's Parliament of Religions, the major convocation at the World's Columbian Exposition, the religion exhibit at the Century of Progress was designed to show how the world's religions 'ha[d] met the challenges of rapid changes.' Although the Hall of Religion had an array of relics, including the famous Chalice of Antioch, its main focus was contemporary and ecumenical, with displays on areas in which different denominations could co-operate and on various religious welfare organizations, such as the Salvation Army, the Near East Foundation, and a number of Jewish service associations. More intellectual religious activities were carried on at the Haskell Institute of Religions, part of the University of Chicago and a legacy of the World's Columbian Exposition.[13]

The federal government spent approximately $450,000 of its $1 million budget to plan, construct, and install exhibits in the Federal Building and in space utilized in the Travel and Transport Building, the Hall of Science, and the Hall of Social Science. Under the supervision of Commissioner Harry New and Assistant Commissioner W. B. Causey, and with the advice of Martin Jenter, a professional exhibit consultant from New York, the federal government exhibits, for the most part, followed the guidelines of the fair management to show process rather than product. The most visible federal exhibit, however, was the army encampment, sponsored by the War and Navy Departments, on nearly six acres located near the housing exhibit north of the Travel and Transport Building. Camp John Whistler, named for the commander of old Fort Dearborn, was temporary home to 436 men from both the navy and the army, including units of cavalry and artillery. Beyond their daily routine of drilling and maintaining their site, the troops provided honor guards for visits of dignitaries; normally, a cavalry escort would meet the guest outside the Court of Honor, infantry units would parade in, and the artillery would fire the appropriate salute. The highlight of naval participation was a sham battle conducted on Navy Day, 27 October 1933.[14]

Other exhibits were more traditional. The Agriculture Department which with the Commerce Department was allocated the largest share of the exhibit budget, occupied 6,500 square feet on the ground floor of the Federal Building. Its display of scenic settings, dioramas, specimens, maps and charts, lights, and things that moved illustrated the history and activities of the eighteen branches of the department, ranging from the Agricultural Adjustment Agency, a New Deal measure, to the Weather Bureau. There was emphasis placed on the idea of 'Adjusting Agriculture to Fit Today's Conditions,' and over 30,000 copies of a free booklet, 'Science Serving Agriculture,' were distributed.[15]

The Commerce Department, which was composed of an even greater and more varied array of branches than the Agriculture Department, spread its exhibit out over nearly 7,200 square feet in the Federal Building, with other displays in the Hall of Science, the Travel and Transport Building, and the Adler Planetarium. Among the more popular exhibits were the Census Bureau's population clock, which recorded the up-to-the-minute estimated US population and the Fisheries Bureau's freshwater fish pool, complete with live fish, rocks, evergreens, and a model of a fish ladder.[16]

Several of the smaller government agencies participating had some of the more noteworthy exhibits. The National Park Service built as its centerpiece a 20 foot by 8 foot by 11-foot high model of Mt Rainier, with lights of changing intensity and color that showed its appearance at various hours of the day or night. By pressing a button, visitors could create a snowstorm on the mountain, which was situated in a booth framed with live trees taken from Mt Rainier Park. The exhibit for the territory of Alaska featured five scenic dioramas and 'Slim' Williams, a native Alaskan who traveled ten months by dogsled to get to Chicago. He set up camp in a model of a typical Alaska cabin and remained at the fair through the 1934 season. The Panama Canal Administration built a model of the canal that was nearly 13 feet long by 5 feet wide and distributed 30,000 copies of a pamphlet, 'The Panama Canal: A National Achievement in a Century of Progress.'[17]

One of the most popular government exhibits, attracting a million visitors in 1933, was that of the National Advisory Committee for Aeronautics. It included a number of moving displays showing how airplanes fly and how pilots control airplanes in flight. The exhibit also included a full-scale wind tunnel model, and a water tank for testing seaplane hulls. On the other hand, the Smithsonian Institution, which, for many past fairs had been responsible for the US exhibits, found itself outclassed with its static display of oil paintings showing past Smithsonian expeditions and a slide show depicting current Smithsonian activities.[18]

There was only one major difficulty between federal authorities and the fair management. In May 1933, three weeks before Opening Day, the Secretary of the Interior, Harold Ickes, pulled the Bureau of Indian Affairs exhibit from the Maya Temple after he learned that a 'commercialised' Indian village was to be built just outside the temple. Ickes felt that the live Indians in the village would badly undermine the effectiveness of the bureau's exhibit of Indian relics and pictures. Fay Cooper-Cole, the director of social science exhibits, assured Ickes that the live Indian 'village' would be anthropologically correct, the dances and pageants would be accurately staged and 'devoid of all wild west features.'[19]

Because of the continuing economic crisis, only twenty-two states and Puerto Rico participated in the 1933 Century of Progress, and only Illinois had its own pavilion. Many states simply did not have the funds available to send exhibits to Chicago. The Massachusetts legislature, for example, voted down a Century of Progress appropriations bill for $25,000 and passed a resolution declaring that any excess funds should go to relieve the unemployed. Of the various state exhibits, that of Illinois, the host state, was the most elaborate. The state legislature appropriated $350,000 in 1933 and another $100,000 in 1934, for the construction and maintenance of the Illinois State Building (or Illinois Host House, as it was frequently called), and the state's exhibit in the building. The Illinois Building, with its 70-foot central tower, was situated near the center of the fairgrounds, and contained three rooms devoted to an Abraham Lincoln exhibit, as well as lounges for visitors, offices, and an auditorium. In addition, Illinois exhibits could be found in the Agricultural Building, the Hall of States, and the Hall of Science.

Of the other state exhibits, Indiana's aroused the most controversy. An exhibit devoted entirely to culture, its main feature was a mural painted by noted American artist Thomas Hart Benton which some visitors felt carried a hostile political message ('socialist preachments') seen in the depiction of a sign held by a miner, 'Workers, why vote the rich man's ticket?' Defenders of the mural said that Benton was not a socialist but was just trying to represent accurately Indiana's heritage, seen also in parts of the mural that showed a Ku Klux Klan rally and a hospital scene showing a black child getting free treatment from a white medical staff. Organizers were relieved when the number of visitors exceeded their expectation, thus justifying their decision to create a cultural display.[20]

Michigan's more traditional exhibit contained murals of Michigan history, examples of furniture made in Grand Rapids, and dioramas of a furniture factory, a paper mill, and an automobile plant. The main reception room included a 10-foot high waterfall with water chilled to 52 degrees to cool the air in the room, simulated trees typical of Michigan forests, and dioramas of Michigan vacation scenes. Fourteen guides were employed to answer visitors' questions and maintain the appearance of the pavilion.

Among other state exhibits, Ohio's featured a large map with lights indicating the location of every city and town. New York displayed Edward Steichen's photographs and Joseph Urban's panoramas, while Georgia's exhibit included four golf balls used by Bobby Jones to win golf's four major tournaments in 1930.[21]

Among the foreign participants, Japan and Sweden, both of which had their own pavilion, had distinctive exhibits. The Japanese pavilion, located near the Sky-Ride, contained a collection of Japanese art and industrial products valued at $3 million. In addition, there was a large map sent by the South Manchurian Railway, a $500,000 scale model of Mt Vernon made by Japanese craftsmen from shells and pearls, a silk-weaving demonstration with live workers, and a tea room for weary visitors. For their part, the Swedes emphasized the need to develop 'products for everyday life' rather than luxury goods. Swedish manufacturers, therefore, exhibited high quality goods manufactured by mass production techniques. This kind of exhibit, it was noted, had been highly criticized at the 1930 Stockholm exposition, just before the impact of the depression was noticeable, but by 1933, the criticism had died away, and the exhibit was well received.[22]

One of the most highly regarded smaller foreign exhibits was that of the Philippines, located on the second floor of the Travel and Transport Building. The Philippines had spent $150,000 on their exhibit at the 1931 Paris Colonial Exhibition and had won first prize for it; the legislature appropriated the same amount for the Chicago fair, but the governor vetoed the bill, and the exhibit was prepared at much less cost by the Philippine Tourist Association. The small display featured a variety of Filipino arts and crafts, muslin made from pineapple fiber, and four friendly guides, all graduates of the University of the Philippines.[23]

In practical terms, the model housing exhibit, developed and co-ordinated by the Century of Progress management and executed by private builders, was a nearly ideal expression of the theme of the fair. In the eleven model homes that were constructed, and in the nearby Home and Industrial Arts pavilion, visitors could see where science and technology had taken domestic life in America. For the most part, these were 'new, common-sense' homes, falling in between elegant mansions affordable only by the very wealthy and tract homes, thrown up for sheer commercial expediency without any concern for esthetic values.

The book published in conjunction with the model homes noted four essential features shared by the structures. First, the homes were durable, employing the 'most nearly indestructable construction elements yet known.' Second, the homes were convenient, equipped with all the latest labor-saving devices. Third, the homes were livable, expressing beauty and a 'quiet, restful harmony,' with simple and subtle décor. Finally, and perhaps most importantly in economically troubled times, the homes were relatively inexpensive, incorporating such features as automatic central heating and cooling and 'scientific space usage,' which would cut the costs of construction.[24]

The idea of a homes exhibit was suggested to Raymond Hood of the

Architectural Commission by Allen Albert in March 1928, soon after the commission was formed. In February 1929, N. Max Dunning and Eugene H. Klaber submitted a report to Albert and the Architectural Commission outlining a proposal for a homes exhibit. Dunning and Klaber thought that this would be an important exhibit, since homes affect everybody, and that therefore it should be treated differently from any other industrial exhibit. They proposed that a small village be built as a kind of setting for the model homes. Located on the south end of Northerly Island, this village would have streets, public buildings, and a town center, which would include related exhibits on such topics as town planning and zoning, gardening, and building financing. Dunning and Klaber also suggested that European architects should be involved in the model homes exhibit, since this was an important topic of concern there, and it would help secure European participation in the exposition. The two architects were no doubt pleased when the Architectural Commission approved their general plan in June, noting that such an exhibit could be 'one of the most influential and entertaining features' of the fair.[25]

Dunning and Klaber continued to refine their scheme, and in February 1930, they presented a fairly detailed sketch to the Architectural Commission. The model village, at the south end of the island, would be at the foot of the bridge across the lagoon. At one end of the village, a residential area, consisting of a town house section, a single family dwelling section, and a foreign section, would be built, while at the opposite end, there would be a school and playground. Finally, along the lake side of the village, a public garden area would be planted. Although Dunning and Klaber did not specify any particular number of model homes, they felt that a village of lesser size and scope than specified in their proposal would 'spoil [the] effectiveness' of the entire exhibit. On the basis of this work, the board of trustees contracted with the two as consulting architects for the model housing project at $30 per day plus expenses and overhead.[26]

It was not long before the realities of the depression caught up with the elaborate plans of Dunning and Klaber. In August 1931, they were told that there would be eight different homes built by eight different builders, each one distinctive in style and material. Instead of a model village with a town center and other public spaces, an exhibition hall would be built for presentations of town planning and the like, and Dunning and Klaber were asked to draw up some suggestions for items to display in that hall. In July 1932, the two architects were advised that the fair was short on cash and would be able to pay them only $30 each for one day's work, although they later asked for and received additional pay.[27]

Although Dunning and Klaber were eased out for financial reasons, the model homes exhibit continued to develop, with fair officials like J. C. Folsom working directly with individual builders. The location of the model homes was moved from Northerly Island to a site in between the Midway and the military encampment. In addition, a Home and Industrial Arts pavilion, designed by Ely Jacques Kahn of New York, was built south of Fort Dearborn and the Midway adjacent to the model homes. This building was an 'I'-shaped structure, two-stories tall at either end, with a series of galleries through the center. Exhibits of glassware, silver, leather, metals, fine woods, and draperies were displayed in the galleries, while one end of the pavilion contained a series of furnished rooms, and the other showcased the latest in appliances and household equipment such as air conditioning and insulating materials. Kahn noted that this kind of exhibit was in the character of recent European expositions, such as the Paris Decorative Arts exposition of 1925, but was new to American fairs.[28]

Next to the Homes and Industrial Arts pavilion were eleven model homes. Eight of these were 'delightful' small houses designed to be economical residences that in different ways showed the possibilities of prefabricated units and new building materials yet retained variety of style and individuality in taste. Two other homes, a Florida home with emphasis on modernity and a classically-designed home displaying period furniture, were part of the exhibit but were clearly intended to be more expensive dwellings. Finally, an eleventh home – the scientific home of the future called the 'House of Tomorrow' – was billed as a 'daring conception, inside and out.'

Designed by Chicago architect George Fred Keck, the House of Tomorrow was a twelve-sided two-story glass and steel house, with many windows that did not open, owing to the central air conditioning. A central pillar supported the house and served as a chase for wiring, plumbing, and gas lines. Everything in the house was waterproof and fireproof. The floors were of walnut and brick, coated with Bakelite to protect them against burning and staining. The inside partitions were Carrera glass, and the house had movable wardrobes rather than closets.

The ground level was conceived as a work and play level, with a complete workshop, garage, airplane hangar, and laundry. In addition, there was a recreation room with a tile floor, metal furniture, and a small bar for the 'drinks of tomorrow.' The ceiling consisted of nothing more than steel beams and the floor of the upper story. One climbed to the upper story by means of a circular stairway in the center of the house. On that level was a living-dining room with chairs like automobile seats on chrome frames and modern wood tables cut from one piece of elegant tropical wood. The dining-room table was made of Bakelite-finished wood on chrome legs that could be divided to make two card tables. The kitchen was all stainless steel, porcelain, and glass. The bedrooms, which could be made private by the use of curtains, Venetian blinds, or aluminum-backed shades, contained metal beds, but wooden furniture otherwise and wooden floors. In the children's bedroom, there was a piece of furniture that served as a bookcase and locker during the day and opened into two beds at night. On the roof was a glass solarium with canvas gliders on chrome frames, and a sundeck just outside. Built without regard to cost, the House of Tomorrow was billed as a 'laboratory' house, and visitors were surveyed to determine which features they found most attractive.[29]

Several of the more modest residences were notable for new materials or new building techniques. The Stran-Steel House, built by Carl A. Strand, a Michigan contractor, had exterior walls of prefabricated enameled steel plates attached to a steel frame. The Rostone House was built with a new material, called Rostone, made from pressed pulverized limestone and shale which could be molded and colored to the client's specification. The Armco-Ferro Enamel House had no frame at all but was built of pre-fabricated box-like units that had doors and windows welded in place and could be fitted together like children's building blocks. Another completely prefabricated house was that displayed by Howard Fisher of General Homes. This house, available in several models, had a prefabricated frame and wall units and could be erected in a very short time. In keeping with the theme of the fair, each of Fisher's models had a name that resembled a chemical formula. But the houses looked so boxy and industrial that they proved unpopular. It is difficult to know what any of these houses would have cost on the open market, but Carl Strand reported that the Stran-Steel House had cost $10,000 to erect, and another $5,000 for operation and maintenance during the exposition.[30]

Regardless of the method employed, the object of the exhibits was to 'educate you so painlessly you will not realize you are being educated.' And it seems to have worked. The magazine *Business Week*, not usually given to exuberant commentary, concluded that the emphasis on process makes exhibits that would normally be boring 'graphic and interesting . . . , a great demonstration of applied showmanship.'[31]

There were no special pavilions for exhibits of women or minorities. Helen Bennett, assistant to the director of the social science exhibits, reported that many with whom she had spoken had said that a woman architect should design a women's pavilion, as had been the case at the World's Columbian Exposition, and that women's achievements as a group should 'have quarters of their own.' She also suggested an exhibit on the changing status of women over the past century. The fact that the Century of Progress had no women's building and that exhibits of women's accomplishments were confined to the federal government's Department of Labor display probably says more about the general state of the women's movement than about any parochial anti-feminism on the part of Rufus Dawes and Lenox Lohr. For the record, Dawes wrote years after the fair, commenting about a critical article in the *Women's Home Companion*, 'it was . . . the decision of the women of Chicago that so much progress had been made in cooperation between men and women that emphasis ought to be placed on this cooperation rather than on their distinctive fields of activity.' Although there was nothing equivalent to the World's Congress of Representative Women at the Century of Progress, both the National Federation of Business and Professional Women and the National Council of Women held their 1933 conventions in Chicago because of the allure of the fair, and in 1933 and 1934, the Chicago Women's Club sponsored series of lectures at the Illinois Host House on issues of concern to women.[32]

The fair board had a clearly stated anti-discrimination policy and had erected a replica of the house of Jean Baptiste Point du Sable, a French-speaking black man generally acknowledged to have been Chicago's first resident. With respect to commercial exhibits, blacks could apply for exhibit space on the same terms as anyone else. Here, however, Sewell's southern heritage got in the way. In August 1931, a group of Africans submitted a proposal for an exhibit, and a worried Sewell asked Dr Howard W. Odum, director of social science exhibits, to look it over, because, Sewell wrote, 'it might develop into an effort at Negro propaganda.' In December, Sewell reported to Lohr that various 'groups of Negroes' had come to him looking for ways in which they could participate. Some were 'smart niggers . . . , looking for easy money for themselves,' while others were natives of Africa, university students, who should be encouraged to develop an exhibit dealing with African contributions to scientific progress. Evidently Sewell was not very encouraging, because there is no further record of black efforts to exhibit until January 1933, after Sewell's resignation.

In that month, a group of Chicago blacks formed the All-Africa Corporation and signed a contract to provide an exhibit of the life of the peoples of Africa. On $15,000 worth of space, the All-Africa Corporation planned an ambitious exhibit that included two museums (African art and American Negro displays), a native *kraal* with fifty African natives living in huts, space for traditional dances and ceremonies, and some added attractions such as fortune tellers and snake charmers. The corporation hoped to get its investment back and make a profit by charging twenty cents admission, but it forfeited its contract on 18 April for failing to submit detailed plans and begin work by the 1 February deadline or have the exhibit under roof by 15 April.[33]

Although scientific progress over the past century was the theme of the fair, organizers knew that every respectable world's fair in the past had included a fine arts exhibit. Indeed, the Museum of Science and Industry, which had only recently opened its doors to Chicagoans, had been the Fine Arts building for the World's Columbian Exposition. In the planning for that fair, some thought had been given to placing exhibits of painting and sculpture at the Art Institute, built in 1891 on Michigan Avenue, adjacent to downtown Chicago. But it had been decided that Michigan Avenue was too far away from Jackson Park for the Art Institute to be useful, and so a Fine Arts building was constructed on the site.

The Art Institute, a first-class museum, was much closer to the site of the Century of Progress, however, and from the beginning, it was generally assumed that the fine arts exhibits would be developed in connection with the Art Institute and shown there. On 5 September 1928, Chauncey McCormick raised that possibility at a board of trustees meeting, and the board passed it on to the architectural commission, which endorsed it three months later, suggesting also that the fair provide transportation between the site and the Art Institute.[34]

There was some discussion in the architectural commission in early 1930 that if the Art Institute could not meet the needs of the Century of Progress by means of a proposed expansion program, then the fair would have to build its own fine arts pavilion, probably near the Hall of Science at 16th Street. But with the coming of the depression and the knowledge that such a pavilion would be quite expensive, given the fireproofing and security needs, such discussion was quietly dropped, and in June 1932, a formal agreement between the Art Institute and the fair board was signed. This authorized the Art Institute to provide and manage an art exhibit in the name of the exposition. The institute staff, headed by Dr Robert B.

Harshe, would select and display the paintings and sculpture, and the fair agreed to sponsor no other significant art exhibit. The institute would absorb all expenses incurred in mounting the show, but the Century of Progress agreed to give the institute 20 per cent of any surplus funds after the end of the fair.[35]

The 1933 art exhibit at the Art Institute attracted just over 700,000 visitors at twenty-five cents each during its five-month run, about half the total number of visitors to the institute during that period of time. What visitors saw for their quarter was an exhibit based on the theme 'A Century of Progress in American Collecting,' consisting of an array of artworks, borrowed from twenty-five museums and over 200 American private collections. There was no limitation on the subjects of the art; it ranged from Italian primitives to contemporary abstract painting. The only piece that did not come from the United States was James MacNeill Whistler's familiar portrait of his mother, borrowed from the Louvre museum in Paris.

Although the distance between the Art Institute and the fairgrounds limited the number of visitors who saw the fine arts exhibits in 1933 and 1934, those who did see them were favorably impressed. Critics applauded the rapid improvement in the level of American taste in fine art since the World's Columbian Exposition, but perhaps to many less sophisticated viewers, the classic works of art represented no more than a quiet permanence of beauty, in contrast to the innovative fair architecture that loudly suggested transition and change.[36]

For a great number of visitors to the Century of Progress, the various scientific and cultural exhibits were a veritable education, even if, as Bruce Bliven suggested, few were able to remember much of what they saw. But just as Charles Dudley Arnold's photographs of the World's Columbian Exposition suggest that there the Midway was more popular than the industrial exhibits, the numerous concessions at the Century of Progress also drew many visitors away from the educational exhibits.

Notes

1   Quoted in Mildred Adams, 'America goes to the fair: 1893 and 1933,'*New York Times Sunday Magazine*, 17 September 1933.
2   Report of Design Section, COP 15–121.
3   John Stephen Sewell to Lenox Lohr, 18 March 1931, COP 11–11; Trustees' Meeting, 30 June 1932, COP 3–24.

4   Louis Skidmore, 'Planning the exposition displays,' *Architectural Record*, LXXIII, 19 May 1933, pp. 342–46; Sewell memorandum, 'Suggestions for sales force of the exhibits department,' 29 March 1932, COP 11–2; J. Franklin Bell to Evelyn Gordon, 14 November 1934, COP 1–13114.

5   Raymond Hood to Allen D. Albert, 13 March 1928, COP 5–25.

6   COP memorandum, 'Brief summary of report of meeting August 20–21 [1930?] re exhibits,' COP 11–8; Sewell to C. W. Fitch, 3 November 1930, COP 11–11; Sewell to Lohr, 14 February 1931, COP 11–12.

7   Lenox R. Lohr, *Fair Management: The Story of a Century of Progress Exposition*, Chicago, 1952, pp. 121–22; 'An engineer sees the world,' *Power Plant Engineering*, XXXVIII, June 1933, pp. 240–41; 'The queen of the sciences,' *Power Plant Engineering*, XXXVIII, June 1933, pp. 246–47; 'Physics – modern genie of the lamp,' *Power Plant Engineering*, XXXVIII, June 1933, pp. 248–51; 'Chemistry – economic dictator of the future,' *Power Plant Engineering*, XXXVIII, June 1933, pp. 252–55. See also the articles 'Electricity – the silent partner of industry,' and 'Industry – the pulse of the nation,' in the same issue of *Power Plant Engineering*.

    Botany was one science that the Century of Progress exhibits department chose to avoid. Sewell advised C. W. Fitch in November 1930 that it would be impossible to build and maintain a botanical garden, although botanists could show models of plants to illustrate the classification system. Exhibits of live plants were left to the commercial exhibitors in the Horticultural Building. Sewell to Fitch, 1 November 1930, COP 11–11.

8   Bruce Bliven, 'A century of treadmill,' *New Republic*, LXXVII, 15 November 1933, pp. 11–13. By contrast, James O'Donnell Bennett was so impressed with the exhibits in the Electrical Group that he wrote, '[A]nybody who fails to spend at least a day in the Palace of Electricity 'for his own good' is so dumb and lethargic that he ought to go back to the Middle Ages and die there,' *Chicago Tribune*, 14 June 1933.

9   Rufus C. Dawes, *Report of the President of a Century of Progress to the Board of Trustees*, Chicago, 1936, pp. 26–28; Lohr, *Fair Management*, p. 45.

10 'Business and "the fair",' *Business Week*, 31 May 1933, pp. 13–14.

11 J. Parker Van Zandt, 'A miracle in cans,' *Review of Reviews and World's Work*, XC, October 1934, pp. 54–57.

12 'Century dairy exhibit on time,' *Milk Plant Monthly*, XXII, May 1933, pp. 51–52; 'Livestock and dairy industries feature of 1933 exposition,' *Rural Business*, III, November 1932, p. 10; *Chicago Tribune*, 24 June and 7 July 1933.

13 *Chicago Tribune*, 20 May 1933; COP, *Official Guide and Time Saving Trips through the Fair*, Chicago, 1933, pp. 82–84.

14 Martin Jenter file, COP Papers, RG 43, Entry 1392, Box 7, National Archives; Final Report 1933, COP Papers, RG 43, Entry 1392, Box 6, National Archives; Memorandum re space utilization by US government exhibits [October 1932], COP Papers, RG 43, Entry 1392, Box 1, National Archives. A number of the more distinctive government exhibits are surveyed in George Dacy, 'Uncle Sam's scientists display their contributions to progress at great world's fair,' *Popular Science Monthly*, CXXII, June 1933, pp. 9–11, 95.

15 Report of Department of Agriculture exhibit, 1934, COP Papers, RG 43, Entry 1393, Box 1, National Archives.

16 Report of Department of Commerce exhibit, 1934, COP Papers, RG 43, Entry 1393, Box 1, National Archives.

17 Press Release, COP, 26 January 1933, COP Papers, RG 43, Entry 1392, Box 12; Report on Department of Interior exhibit, COP Papers, RG 43, Entry 1393, Box 3; Report on Panama Canal exhibit, COP papers, RG 43, Entry 1393, Box 5, National Archives.

18 Report of National Advisory Committee for Aeronautics, 8 January 1934, COP Papers, RG 43, Entry 1394, Box 1, National Archives; Report of Smithsonian Institution, 1934, COP Papers, RG 43, Entry 1394, Box 1, National Archives.

19 *Chicago Tribune*, 16 May 1933; E. K. Burlew to Harry E. New, 6 May 1933; COP Papers, RG 43, Entry 1393, Box 3, National Archives; Fay Cooper-Cole to Harold Ickes, 8 May 1933, COP Papers, RG 43, Entry 1393, Box 3, National Archives.

20 Mary Q. Burnet, 'Indiana at the world's fair,' *American Magazine of Art*, XXVI, August 1933, p. 390; *Chicago Tribune*, 3 May, 7 and 8 June 1933; W. B. Causey to Harriet M. Sweet, 7 January 1935, COP Papers, RG 43, Entry 1393, Box 1, National Archives.

21 *Chicago Tribune*, 9 June 1933.

22 *Chicago Tribune*, 6 June 1933; Bengt Theodor Lundberg, 'Arts and crafts at the Swedish Chicago exposition 1933,' pamphlet at du Pont Library, Winterthur Institute, Winterthur, Delaware.

23 *Chicago Tribune*, 16 October 1933.

24 Dorothy Raley (ed.), *A Century of Progress Homes and Furnishings*, Chicago, 1934, pp. 5–7.

25 Allen D. Albert to Raymond Hood, 15 March 1928, COP 5–25; N. Max Dunning and Eugene H. Klaber to Allen D. Albert, 28 February 1929, COP 1–4863.

26 Albert to Dunning and Klaber, 4 June 1929, COP 1–4863; Dunning and Klaber memorandum attached to sketch plan of housing exhibit, 1 February 1930, COP 5–426; COP to Dunning, 16 April 1931[?], COP 1–4863.

27 Nathaniel Owings to Dunning, 26 August 1931, COP 1–4863; Daniel H. Burnham to Dunning and Klaber, 14 July 1932, COP 1–4863.

28 Barbara Niles, 'Century of Progress,' *Design*, XXXIV, July 1932, p. 68; Bryan Holme, 'Forceful architecture at Chicago's world's fair,' *Commercial Art and Industry*, XV, October 1933, pp. 136–42.

29 Press release, COP, 15 August 1933, COP 15–150; Lohr, *Fair Management*, p. 134.

30 J. C. Folsom to Carl A. Strand, 18 July 1932, COP 1–14192; Folsom to Department of Operations and Maintenance, 18 October 1932, COP 1–14192; C. P. Vary to C. W. Fitch, n.d., COP 1–14190; Joseph Corn and Brian Horrigan, *Yesterday's Tomorrows: Past Visions of the American Future*, New York, 1984, pp. 70–73; Lohr, *Fair Management*, p. 133. See also Rosemarie Haag Bletter, 'The world of tomorrow: the future with a past,' in Elaine Koss (ed.), *High Styles: Twentieth Century American Design*, New York, 1986, pp. 84–127.

31 Robert I. Randolph, 'Call victory 1933,' *American Legion Monthly*, XIV, February 1933, pp. 22–23; Business and "the fair",' *Business Week*, 31 May 1933, pp. 11–12.

32 *Chicago Tribune*, 4 and 9 July 1933, 27 May 1934; Dawes to Anna Dunlap, 23 April 1937, COP 15–1. As early as 1929, the American Cosmetologists' Association passed a resolution to support the Century of Progress. Its president, Mrs M. B. McGavran, stated that 'this industry composed largely of women should take a prominent part in the exposition . . . . [W]e believe the cosmetics section in the exhibits building will constitute a real temple of beauty.' Scrapbook of clippings, *c.* 1929, BBC, Box 19.

33 Sewell to Dr Odum, 22 August 1931, COP 11–18; Sewell to Lohr, 22 December 1931, COP 11–14; All-Africa Corporation file, COP 1–190. August Meier and Elliott

M. Rudwick, 'Negro protest at the Chicago world's fair 1933–1934,' *Journal of the Illinois State Historical Society, LIX*, Summer 1966, pp. 162–63; Barbara Holt, 'An American dilemma on display . . . ,' pp. 5–6. The Lincolnshire Country Club, a private golf club for whites only located thirty miles south of Chicago near Crete, Illinois, offered its facilities to Century of Progress visitors who were members of clubs elsewhere. When the fair management asked Lincolnshire how it would handle black golfers, since the fair had a policy forbidding racial discrimination, the club said that it would refer blacks to Jackson Park or Lincoln Park, two city courses that catered to blacks, or to a black tourist office on Woodlawn Avenue that could refer them to courses open to 'colored golf players.' This response satisfied the fair management, which agreed to make Lincolnshire's literature available at its information bureaus. See Lincolnshire C. C. file, COP 1–9378.

34 Trustees' Meeting, 7 December 1928, COP 3–40.

35 Minutes of eighth Architectural Commission meeting, 17–19 March 1930, COP 5–40; Trustees' Meeting, 16 January 1929, COP 3–54; 'Individual masterpieces,' *American Magazine of Art*, XXVI, June 1933, p. 279; 'Another great art exhibit for world's fair,' *Literary Digest*, CXVIII, 4 August 1934, p. 24. In addition to the exhibition at the Art Institute, there were a number of small art shows on the fairgrounds. These included a national miniature exhibition in the graphic arts pavilion in General Exhibits Hall #1, a photography exhibit in the same hall, a show sponsored by the Association of Chicago Painters and Sculptors, in the Home Planning Hall, and another local show, sponsored by the Chicago Society of Painters, on display in the Kroch Gallery in the General Exhibits Hall. *Chicago Tribune*, 2 July 1933.

36 Robert B. Harshe, 'The Century of Progress exhibition of fine arts,' *School Arts*, XXXIII, October 1933, pp. 76–80; Clarence J. Bulliet, 'A century of progress in collecting,' *Parnassus*, V, May 1933, pp. 1–7; 'The significance of the Century of Progress art exhibition,' *Bulletin of the Art Institute of Chicago*, XXVII, September 1933, pp. 81–89. This article states that the artwork in the exhibition was borrowed from thirty-two museums and 156 private collections. Dudley C. Watson, 'What Chicago learned,' *American Magazine of Art*, XXVII, February 1934, pp. 77–79; *New York Times Sunday Magazine*, 17 September 1933; *Chicago Tribune*, 30 and 31 October, 1 and 2 November 1933; Trustees' Meeting, 5 April 1934, COP 3–54.

9   Fun at the fair

> One HUN-dred DOL-lars to you, I don't care WHO you are, reformer or censor, or what-not, if this little lady wears so much as one shred or particle of clothing of any sort what soEVER when she steps upon the stage.[1]

By 1933, the concept of a Midway, or entertainment zone, had become a staple feature of world's fairs. First popularized at the World's Columbian Exposition, the midway came to be widely recognized as a place where visitors weary of serious industrial and agricultural exhibits could find refuge among a mindless melange of rides, games of chance or skill, freak shows, and night club acts that often tested the moral limits of the time and place.

For the Century of Progress organizers, midway traditions posed something of a dilemma. They were trying to bring off a high-minded, educational exposition, based on a theme of science and progress; sleazy midway acts would certainly detract from that goal. On the other hand, they were well aware that their fair had to have broad public appeal in order to be successful; sleazy midway acts would probably contribute to that goal. In the end, they took the most reasonable course by sponsoring some entertainment programs themselves, which were generally faithful to the educational objectives of the fair, while at the same time, they rented space to commercial operations, which, for the most part, sponsored entertainment that was meant to be nothing more than fun. The concessions were especially important for the evening operations of the fair, when the 'spending crowd' came. Exhibit halls were closed by 9.00 p.m., and there was always concern that not enough was being done to attract night-time visitors. Some fair officials suggested closing the free buildings earlier or having concessionaires publicize themselves with free shows, while others urged more publicity or a liberalization of the neon sign policy to create a livelier ambience at night.

Among the fair-sponsored concessions, Fort Dearborn and the Golden Temple of Jehol were open to the public during the summer of 1932,

118

when the fair board fixed a general admission to the grounds at ten cents. Some 600,000 people toured the site, watched the exposition being constructed, and visited the few buildings and concessions that had been finished. Fort Dearborn was a replica of the structure that was built when Chicago was founded, while the Golden Temple of Jehol (also called the Lama Temple) was a replica of a Chinese religious building that had been constructed in 28,000 pieces in China, broken down for shipment to Chicago, and then meticulously reassembled for the fair. Both were popular attractions in 1932, and purchasers of advance tickets to the Century of Progress found special stubs in their ticket books that entitled them to free admission to Fort Dearborn and the Lama Temple in 1933. Thus in 1933, only 20 per cent of the visitors to Fort Dearborn and 46 per cent of those seeing the temple paid cash to enter.[2]

The director of concessions was Dr Forrest R. Moulton, a former chairman of astronomy at the University of Chicago, who had also worked in the public utility sector prior to the Century of Progress. A man of unquestioned integrity, Moulton was responsible for overseeing the construction of those concessions sponsored by the exposition and for arranging contracts with private concessionaires. In the second year of the fair, Nathaniel Owings took over the post. Shortly before the opening day, a division of special features was created, headed by A. N. Gonsior. The task of this unit was to supervise concessions, make certain that concessionaires were living up to their contractural obligations, and deal with any legal, moral, or social problems. Most problems involved so-called 'skill' games that in actuality were more like gambling operations and had to be closed down. The special unit wasted little time. One attraction, 'Rolling Balls,' was shut down within ten days of the opening of the fair after it was found that the operator could determine who, if anyone, could win.

Other problems were raised by concessions that featured dancing or posing by nearly nude performers. These shows made good money and spawned imitators, but frequently raised the ire of so-called 'reformers,' and ran afoul of the law. Gonsior's office did not make arrests, but it was authorized to close objectionable shows. It was not an easy task for Gonsior, who found himself caught between the reformers, who wanted him to act as a moral censor on their behalf, and the concessionaires, who felt that the exposition was being entirely too restrictive of their activities. Still another problem was the noise caused by the loudspeakers used to lure visitors into a particular attraction. One blaring loudspeaker begat another,

23 General View, showing the Sky Ride. The Sky-Ride, although grossly out of scale with the other structures at the Century of Progress, was a popular attraction for fairgoers.

24 The Golden Temple of Jehol, also known as the Bendix Lama Temple, was a replica of an eighteenth century summer home for the Manchu emperors of China. It was brought to the Century of Progress in 28,000 numbered pieces and assembled on the site.

25 In keeping with the historical theme of the Century of Progress (1933), fair managers constructed a replica of Fort Dearborn, which stood on the site of Chicago in 1833.

26 The Abraham Lincoln group consisted of several structures including this reproduction of the cabin in which the notable president was born. One of the few historical exhibits at the fair, it celebrated the life of Illinois' most famous citizen.

27 The Havoline thermometer, located near the 23rd Street entrance to the fairgrounds, stood 240 feet tall and was a familiar Century of Progress landmark.

28 One of eleven model homes at the Century of Progress, this example, called 'Design for Living,' cost $4,000 to build in 1933. John Moore, of New York, was the architect.

29 The Adler Planetarium was presented as 'a miracle of scientific achievement,' and 'the only one in America.'

and so on, until the cacophony on the midway was the source of constant complaint. Ultimately, the problem had to be dealt with in an arbitrary way by the fair's electrical engineer, J. L. McConnell, who was empowered to compel operators to reduce the sound level or have their speaker wires cut.[3]

Of the several fair-sponsored attractions, Wings of a Century, an outdoor pageant on the history of transportation, was by far the most spectacular and the one that most closely complemented the theme of the fair. The idea for this show came from Edward Hungerford, the director of the Fair of the Iron Horse, held in Baltimore in 1927, which had featured a transportation pageant. Dawes heard about it and decided that something like it would be well suited for the Century of Progress. Hungerford was hired as a consultant to Helen Tieken, the pageant director.

A large theater was built near the Travel and Transport Building to stage Wings of a Century. A grandstand seating 3,000 spectators faced a 250-foot forward stage and an 85-foot upper stage. Almost 3,800 feet of railroad track was laid on the forward stage to accommodate the eleven locomotives of different vintages. In addition, the pageant used a dozen carts and wagons, eight to ten automobiles, fifty-five horses, two airplanes including a replica of the Wright brothers' plane, several bicycles, and five boats. It was the 'largest aggregation of agents of transportation that Chicago had ever seen.'

In and amongst all these 'agents of transportation,' a cast of 203 staged an hour-long dramatic presentation in five scenes, a prologue, and an epilogue. Two narrators told the story of the progress of transportation, while the actors silently portrayed the story on stage. One noteworthy feature was the employment of old-time train engineers to run the old locomotives in the pageant. Wings of a Century, described as 'without question . . . the outstanding spectacle and attraction' of the Century of Progress, was a very popular operation, especially after July, when its reputation had spread and it had received excellent critical reviews. Nevertheless, because of the high costs of production, it remained a marginally unprofitable show but one that the fair board thought was well worth the losses.[4]

Another attraction that was designed to augment the educational mission of the fair was The World a Million Years Ago, a scientifically accurate presentation of mechanically animated prehistoric animals, reptiles, and 'Man Before the Dawn of History.' This show utilized a new technology of animation, produced by the New York firm of Messmore and Damon, the 'foremost builders of mechanical displays.' There was much interest in this technique which some thought would be the wave of the future in educational exhibits in museums.

The animated show was staged in a globe-shaped building to symbolize the earth. The inside was decorated like a prehistoric jungle and equipped with a 'moving sidewalk' to facilitate the flow of visitors. What they saw was a series of five large dioramas showing different prehistoric eras and the creatures of those times. Sound effects were added to create a greater illusion of life in the dioramas, and the New York Museum of Natural History supplied the scientific data to help the show achieve accuracy. Visitors liked it, critics praised it, but The World a Million Years Ago was a financial failure, due apparently to a similar prehistoric show sponsored by the Sinclair Refining Company, to which admission was free.[5]

Most of the private concessions operated in two amusement areas. One, called the Midway, ran south from the 23rd Street entrance to 28th Street, near the model homes exhibit, the military encampment and the north end of the transportation complex, while the other, named the Rainbow Area, occupied the extreme south end of the fairgrounds, down to 39th Street from where the spectacular aurora borealis light display, which gave the area its name, emanated. Most of the more successful concessions were in the more centrally located Midway; indeed, fair management had to make special efforts to get visitors to go to the Rainbow Area.

Near the north end of the Midway, at 23rd Street and Leif Erikson Drive, the main lateral roadway through the site, was the Streets of Paris concession. One of two so-called villages that was highly successful during the 1933 season, the Streets of Paris consisted of a grouping of buildings, streets, and squares representative of Paris, with shops and cafés in the buildings. Created by a group of Chicago investors, the attraction had been built for $300,000 and covered three acres near the 23rd Street entrance, a very convenient location. Some sixty-seven subconcessionaires and 1,324 employees worked in the Streets of Paris, in the Café de la Paix, the largest restaurant, or one of the many bars, game booths, craft shops, snack stands, or places of entertainment, including peep shows with alluring names like 'Mademoiselle from Armentières' and more forthrightly, 'Nudist Colony.' By July 1933, over one million visitors had paid twenty-five cents each to walk the Streets of Paris, and it finished the season as one of the most lucrative concessions.[6]

There was a large dance hall, with 200 taxi dancers ready to dance with visitors for a dime on the 2,500 square foot dance floor, but most people flocked to the Lido, a theater that featured the fan dancing of Sally Rand, without question the most notorious entertainer of the exposition. Concern about lewdness in some of the shows of the Streets of Paris had arisen almost as soon as the Century of Progress had opened, when the Rev. Philip Yarrow, superintendent of the Illinois Vigilance Association, was shocked to see 'nearly nude' women performers, 'smutty' postcards for sale, and taxi dancing. Yarrow was careful to explain that he went to the Streets of Paris only because others had complained to him. The park police investigated, but affairs remained quiet until later in the summer when Sally Rand began performing her fan dance.

Born Helen Gould Beck in rural Missouri, Sally Rand was a model, silent film actress, and vaudevillian before she developed the fan dance that brought her national prominence. The dance was not new in 1933; Rand had been doing similar kinds of performances for at least ten years. In 1923, she told a Junior Chamber of Commerce audience, 'At any rate, I haven't been out of work since the day I took my pants off.'

To do her fan dance, Sally Rand covered her nude body with a 'cosmetic whitewash,' followed by an application of white powder, so that, in her words, 'I look just like a beautiful statue.' Wearing a gauzy drape, she did a stylized dance using two large feathered fans, held on either side of her body. During the performance, she allowed the drape to fall to the floor, and at the end of the dance, she momentarily held the two fans high overhead, revealing her whitened nude body.

In early August, Rand was arrested and charged with giving an 'obscene performance' while dancing at a downtown Chicago theater. She was fined $25 and directed to wear clothes while dancing, but six weeks later, she was arrested again on the same charge, fined $200, and sentenced to a year in jail. There was a vast amount of publicity, and when her conviction was overturned on appeal, she returned, more popular than ever. More than two million people visited the Streets of Paris in 1933, and fair officials admitted that the publicity surrounding the fan dancer had benefited the exposition. In 1934, Rand returned to the Century of Progress, this time with a 'bubble dance,' utilizing a semi-transparent 'bubble' 5 feet in diameter.[7]

The social commentator Bruce Bliven, writing about the fair, noted that a dancer named Faith Bacon had originated the fan dance in the Earl Carroll Vanities Show, and that fan dancing, by 1933, was the rage all over the country; one could even buy fan dancing dolls. But Bliven was cynical towards the sale of sex at the Century of Progress, scolding Dawes for 'tolerating the nudity racket' at the fair and scoffing that most of the performers either did an 'awkward and ugly muscle dance,' wearing large amounts of pink court plaster, or else they posed motionless in demure positions no more revealing than an advertisement in *Vogue* magazine.[8]

The other highly successful village, Picturesque Belgium, or more popularly, the Belgian Village, could not have been more unlike the Streets of Paris. Located quite close to the Streets of Paris, the Belgian Village consisted of replicas of old Belgian houses, streets, and squares, representing different historic periods and styles of architecture. There were shops, restaurants, and cafés, and the principal form of entertainment was folk dancing. Its quiet sedateness was very popular, and its success emboldened several entrepreneurs to build rival villages for the 1934 season, most of which lost considerable amounts of money.[9]

A third village that enjoyed two successful seasons at the Century of Progress was Midget Village. This was an L-shaped site of about 9,000 square feet where a miniature Bavarian city was constructed. Populated by eighty-five authentic midgets, Midget Village (known as Midget City during the 1934 season) had its own town government, shops, and services, as well as a theater where midget entertainers presented singing, dancing, and acrobatic shows. For the 1934 season, more structures were added to the site, which were costly, but Midget Village was one of the few concessions that did better in 1934 than in 1933. When organizers of the 1935 San Diego California-Pacific Exposition inquired about Midget Village, Owings wrote that it was a good, clean show that ranked second or third among all villages in popularity in 1934.[10]

Among other attractions on the Midway and in the Rainbow Area, a few strove for some semblance of scientific authenticity in connection with the theme of the fair. One called Life, for example, depicted several scenes of prehistoric, embryological, and biological life through charts and pictures, but the highlight of the show was a display of 180 real embryos in progressive stages of development, accompanied by a lecture. The American Indian Village, sponsored by the Department of Anthropology at the University of Chicago and really an adjunct of the fair's anthropology exhibit, provided for visitors 200 Indians from six different tribes living in traditional structures. There were totem poles loaned by the Field Museum of Natural History, handicraft and archery exhibitions, a trading post, and a stadium seating 2,500 people where traditional Indian dances and other ceremonies were presented.[11]

By contrast, the Seminole Indian Village, another attraction that had been open in 1932, did have twenty authentic Seminoles living in traditional style, but it also had Princess Zenda, a fortune teller, Captain Kelly, who dived from a 104-foot platform into a tank with 7 feet of water, and alligator wrestling. Even more popular, despite a forty cent admission charge, was the Odditorium, associated with Ripley's Believe It or Not, a popular newspaper feature about incredible physical feats or historical facts. In the Odditorium were ten small stages for exhibitions of various kinds done by thirty-six freaks and exotic performers. A similar show was seen in the Living Wonder Show, an unabashed freak show presented in a circus-like setting, and featuring Mary and Margaret Gibbs, Siamese twins; Johnny Eck, the 'living half boy;' Nils Nelson, the man with rubber skin; and Martha Morris, the armless wonder, among others.[12]

Some concessions emphasized history, and most of these lost money. The Pantheon was a building containing a huge picture, 402 feet long by 45 feet wide, painted by twenty-eight French artists and depicting 6,000 life-sized portraits of heroes and leaders from the World War against a setting of French and Belgian battlefields. The Battle of Gettysburg was an attraction featuring a 404-foot long by 75-foot high cyclorama, or 360 degree painting, of the famous Civil War battle, done under the direction of Paul Phillipotaux soon after the end of the war. And the Abraham Lincoln Exhibit displayed reproductions of a number of buildings prominent in Lincoln's life, such as the cabin where he was born and the auditorium where he was nominated for president in 1860.[13]

But many other attractions pandered to the gullibility or tastelessness of visitors. The Oriental Village had no less than five exotic dancing shows, including one tantalizingly called 'Slave Mart,' while Miss America of 1933 featured a performer on a stage with silk drapes and pillows, among which she 'strikes several poses, exposing her body to the audience.' The Real Two-Headed Baby exhibit, starring a dead baby, had performers dressed as nurses explaining the details of this freak, complete with X-ray plates. The Flea Circus, from New York City, purported to have trained fleas that would kick balls around, jump through hoops, and participate in a chariot race. The Monster Snake Show displayed a number of large pythons and boa constrictors, but the real star was Snakeoid, a man who happily swallowed live snakes and allowed himself to be bitten by rattlesnakes. Darkest Africa featured a variety of 'authentic' African natives, including pygmies and 'cannibals from the Ubangi tribe,' and could conceivably have been at least as elevating as the anthropological exhibits in turn-of-the-century fairs, but the natives mostly walked on fire or ate it, or danced on broken glass. And African Dips was a popular game in which the visitor threw a ball at a target. If he (or she) hit the target, a 'colored man' in a little cage was dropped into a tank of water.[14]

At the far south end of the fairgrounds, aviation held sway. There was an air show, called 'Third of a Century of Progress,' in which a number of planes were exhibited to show the evolution of aviation since the Wright brothers' flight in 1903. The US Army Air Corps also displayed its latest planes. For the more adventurous, the Goodyear Blimp took visitors on rides over the site, although the windy weather frequently grounded the lighter-than-air ship. Nearby was Pal-Waukee Airport, a seaplane base offshore at 31st Street, just south of the General Motors building, where visitors could take sightseeing flights. In 1933, 17,000 did, 70 per cent of whom flew for the first time in their lives. Here the worst tragedy of the exposition happened on 11 June 1933, when the *Northern Light*, a Sikorsky S-33 amphibian plane, crashed in the north-west Chicago suburb of Glenview, killing all nine aboard. The plane had been damaged during an unsuccessful attempt to land on the lake and was attempting to reach the airport near Glenview. It was the worst air disaster in Chicago since 1919. Less than a month later, another tragedy occurred when a parachutist jumped from the wing of a plane before a crowd estimated at 75,000 and plunged to his death in the lake when his parachute did not open. An investigation revealed that the leaper was not the experienced parachutist he was billed as, but a Chicago dishwasher who had never jumped from a plane before, and who had passed himself off to fair officials as a well-known chutist.[15]

For children, the main entertainment venue was a five-acre site on the southern part of Northerly Island in between the Electrical Group and the Horticultural Building called Enchanted Island. It was a very popular attraction, with over three million visitors in 1933 and much favorable commentary in newspapers and magazines. Despite its orientation toward children and their activities, almost 70 per cent of the visitors were adults, who paid ten cents to enter (children under twelve were admitted free).

The idea for Enchanted Island was Moulton's, and the attraction was organized by Nathaniel Owings, with the help of Mrs Kellogg Fairbank, the chairperson of the children's committee. Mrs Fairbank secured the services of Josephine Blackstock, playground director in Oak Park, Illinois, who laid out playgrounds suitable for boys and girls of different age groups; her good work in this led to her appointment as director of Enchanted Island. The Junior League, an organization of Chicago women, agreed to publicize Enchanted Island and its activities in return for a percentage of any profits.

In addition to the playgrounds, Blackstock established a Children's Theater that used amateur acts to draw crowds yet keep costs down. In this she was highly successful; of 250 groups that performed in the theater, only three were professional. Most of the performing groups included children, but about twenty amateur adult groups came and put on performances aimed at a juvenile audience. Blackstock also planned a film program, but when it became necessary to use union projectionists, the cost of the program forced its cancellation.

Enchanted Island also contained an Art Gallery for children's art and handicraft exhibits and a 'Ship of Health,' a center where licensed doctors provided health advice to children and their parents. Other attractions were designed for entertainment. Giant wooden figures, 'as tall as a house,' flanked the entranceway, an 'enormous' mechanical elephant moved its head and trunk for visitors, and a children's zoo featured young animals of many species. There were twenty-one rides costing either five or ten cents each, and there were thirty-four other concessions, ranging from a trained monkey show to the Boy Scouts, available to visitors. Finally, Blackstock and the staff of Enchanted Island scheduled a number of special events, including a Baby Bathing Beauty Contest that attracted 700 contestants under the age of seven, a Doll Contest, a Halloween Contest, and a Grandmother's Day Costume Contest.[16]

From the beginning, Century of Progress organizers were aware that involvement with sports would enhance the popularity of the fair. A study was made of sporting events in conjunction with past fairs, and a committee on sports, headed by Colonel Robert R. McCormick of the *Chicago Tribune*, was appointed in 1928 and soon included almost every prominent figure in midwestern sports. Although a great deal of effort was put forth to attract major interregional college football games and other important sporting events to Soldier Field, the large new stadium just west of the Hall of Science, the results were somewhat disappointing.

The Century of Progress did, however, schedule a large number of smaller events, such as Sunday afternoon speedboat races on the lagoon, which were very popular. And through the efforts of Mayor Kelly, who wanted to see sport as a part of the fair, and Arch Ward, the sports editor of the *Chicago Tribune*, the Century of Progress did serve as the vehicle through which the Major League All-Star Baseball game was inaugurated in 1933, and the All-Star Football game, pitting the professional champions against a college all-star team, was begun in 1934. The all-star baseball game remains an integral part of the baseball season today, while the football game continued to be played until well after World War II.[17]

Not all concessions were entertainment-based. One of the most important concessions, and one that generated the largest number of complaints from fairgoers in 1933, was the pay toilet concession. To save an estimated $300,000 for other construction, the fair board had contracted with an independent operator, Brooks Contracting Company, to build public restrooms on the grounds, with the provision that 80 per cent of the toilets would cost five cents to use and the other 20 per cent would be free. The pay toilets and the free toilets were generally not at the same place, and there were complaints that most of the free toilets were clustered near Soldier Field or the beachfront. In addition, the concessionaire employed restroom attendants on a commission plus tip basis. A visitor could pay ten cents for a linen towel to use; the attendant kept a portion of this as well as any tips he or she received. Restrooms were supposed to be equipped also with free paper towels, but attendants quickly recognized the economic advantage in making the paper towels disappear. The pay toilets and attendants produced many complaints, but fair officials felt that nothing could be done to ameliorate the situation during the 1933 season. For the next season, however, the fair took over restroom management itself and transformed all the toilets into free ones.[18]

The various concessions and entertainment programs were an important element in the financial impact of the fair. The *Chicago Tribune* estimated that as of 1 November 1933, visitors had spent about $35 million in admissions, concessions (including food and drink), and special exhibits on the grounds. Fair records showed that gate receipts accounted for about $8.24 million of that total, with concessions amounting, therefore, to something close to $27 million. Records of individual attractions confirm their popularity. The Streets of Paris grossed $1.465 million, the Sky-Ride, $757,277, and Enchanted Island, $274,062. Crown Foods, which operated forty sandwich stands and six grills on the grounds, reported a gross income of $1.686 million. From the concessions, the Century of Progress received $2.236 million in rents and royalties in 1933 and another $3.184 million in 1934, a total that amounted to about 16 per cent of the fair's revenue over the two years.[19]

In his history of the Century of Progress, Lenox Lohr expressed satisfaction with the nature of the concessions that had been provided for fair visitors. He felt that they had been an important night-time activity after people 'had been instructed' by scientific exhibits during the day. Just as important, perhaps, was the revenue that the Century of Progress derived from its concessions. Fees paid in advance by concessionaires financed the construction of the bridge across the south end of the lagoon at a time when other funds were not available, and the concession stands on the bridge enjoyed a privileged location. In his account, Lohr noted the problems with salacious dancers, obnoxious loudspeakers, and corrupt games, but he defended the fair's policies toward these matters. With the exception of a number of major concessions that experienced critical financial difficulties in the 1934 season, the Century of Progress and its concessionaires worked well together, providing diverse forms of entertainment for fairgoers and a modicum of profit for the operators.[20]

Notes

1   Quoted in Bruce Bliven, 'A century of treadmill,' *New Republic*, LXXVII, 15 November 1933, p. 12.
2   Report of the Executive Committee, Board of Trustees, 21 July 1932, COP 3–22; O. J. F. Keating to Lohr, 23 June 1933, COP 11–4; Memorandum from John McMahon to Farrier, Bartley, Owings, and Bell, 4 August 1934, COP 9–78; A. N. Gonsior, 'Report of the special features division,' pp. 7–11, COP 15–102.
3   Gonsior, 'Report,' pp. 1–6; *Chicago Tribune*, 8 June 1933.
4   Gonsior, 'Report,' pp. 74–76. Nathaniel Owings, 'Amusement features of the exposition,' *Architectural Record*, LXXIII, May 1933, pp. 360–61; Charles Collins, the drama critic of the *Chicago Tribune*, exulted that the Century of Progress was so 'comprehensive in its enchantments . . . that a mere dramatic critic experiences an unaccustomed humility in approaching the theme.' Nevertheless, he collected himself enough to write that Wings of a Century was the most 'elaborate and interesting of all the Century of Progress attractions.' See his review in the *Chicago Tribune*, 2 July 1933.
5   Gonsior, 'Report,' pp. 85–88; Owings, 'Amusement features,' p. 361.
6   *Chicago Tribune*, 7 July 1933.
7   Gonsior, 'Report,' pp. 182–83; *Chicago Tribune*, 7 June, 9 August and 25 September 1933; T. R. Carskadon, 'Sally Rand dances to the rescue,' *American Mercury*, XXXV, July 1935, pp. 355–58. For a droll version of the Sally Rand nudity affair, see the privately printed, anonymous pamphlet, 'A century of nudity,' Chicago, 1933, at the Chicago Historical Society.
8   Bliven, 'Century of treadmill,' p. 12.
9   Gonsior, 'Report,' pp. 181–82.
10 Gonsior, 'Report,' pp. 166–67; Owings to David Larson, 10 October 1934, COP 1–13114.
11 Gonsior, 'Report,' pp. 151–52; 180–81.
12 *Ibid.*, pp. 153–54, 156–57, 167–68.
13 *Ibid.*, pp. 158, 161–62, 169–70.
14 *Ibid.*, pp. 149–51, 152–53, 159–60, 163–64, 166, 168–69; *Chicago Tribune*, 7 July 1933.

15 Gonsior, 'Report,' pp. 177–79; *Chicago Tribune*, 12 June and 5 July 1933. According to Gonsior's report, the concessions collectively took in $1.12 for each paid admission to the fair. Cashiers and ticket takers for concessions were provided by the Century of Progress; 'girls' were paid forty cents per hour, while 'men' received fifty-five cents. See Gonsior, 'Report,' pp. 1–6, and Memorandum on concession regulations, 1933, COP 10–29.

16 Gonsior, 'Report,' pp. 89–93, 98–103; Owings, 'Amusement features,' pp. 358–60; H. W. Magee, 'The enchanted island,' *Popular Mechanics*, LIX, February 1933, pp. 202–16; Rose G. King, 'Enchanted Island,' *Parents*, VIII, June 1933, pp. 31, 59–60.

17 Thomas B. Littlewood, *Arch: A Promoter, Not a Poet. The Story of Arch Ward*, Ames, Iowa, 1990, pp. 67–69, 89–90.

18 Gonsior, 'Report,' p. 6; Lenox R. Lohr, *Fair Management: The Story of a Century of Progress Exposition*, Chicago, 1952, p. 170; *Chicago Tribune*, 23–24 May and 6 November 1933.

19 *Chicago Tribune*, 3 November 1933; Lohr, *Fair Management*, p. 45.

20 Lohr, *Fair Management*, pp. 163–70.

10   A second season: 1934

[It] would be a very fine thing to keep open.[1]

Toward the end of the 1933 season, and particularly after President Franklin Roosevelt's visit on 2 October, there was increasing interest and discussion about reopening the Century of Progress for a second season in 1934. Roosevelt himself alluded to that in a thank you note to Dawes on 11 October, noting that many who had not been able to attend in 1933 would be able to visit in 1934 and promising that he would recommend that Congress appropriate funds to maintain the federal building and exhibits for another year. In late October, exhibitors were asked if they would be interested in returning for a second year, as plans for a renewal of the fair had 'suddenly come to a definite head.' And on 4 November, the *Chicago Tribune* reported that the fair board had voted to reopen the fair the following year, pending support of the Illinois legislature and sufficient commitment from the local business community. The newspaper noted the most important reason for a second season: that the total indebtedness had been reduced to about $5 million, a $21 million plant was already in place, and a second year of the fair would wipe out the remaining debt.[2]

There was little public dissent with the fair board's decision, although privately, Dr Frank B. Jewett of the National Research Council told Dawes that he felt that if the fair were opened for a second year solely for financial reasons, the renewal would be like 'a warmed over dinner.' He added that he would not be able to get scientific organizations to meet in Chicago again and that it would be simply 'a sort of anti-climax' to reopen. Dawes responded that the 1933 season had been very beneficial to Chicago and that the fair was still obligated to its bondholders. Civic support was very strong, the fair buildings were in good condition, and the success of the fair in 1933 had been good for the national spirit.[3]

Indeed, the Century of Progress had been beneficial for Chicago in 1933. The total number of paid admissions was slightly less than 23,000,000. Of that number, fair officials estimated that 9 million visitors came from out of town and spent two days at the fair, for a total of 18 million admissions. The other 5 million came from 500,000 Chicagoans who each went to the fair an average of ten times. During the peak of the 1933 season, 22,000 people were employed at the fair, and one contemporary observer estimated that the fair had been responsible, directly or indirectly, for 100,000 jobs, $400 million of business brought to the city, and an increase of 17 per cent in bank deposits (against a national average increase of 7 per cent). Department store sales increased 19 per cent, turning around a decrease of nearly 25 per cent for the same period in 1932.

According to a Century of Progress press release, Chicago hosted 1,478 conventions in 1933, with a total of just under 1.6 million visitors, more than double the number of conventions and visitors the year before. About 90 per cent of the conventions were held during the period the fair was open. Hotels averaged 60,000 guests per day during the exposition period, an increase of 133 per cent over the preceding year, and total hotel income was estimated at $24.5 million. The average occupancy rate in 1933 was higher than that of 1929, the previous record year. Overall, the city 'came off much better than anyone outside of Chicago dreamed.'[4]

To try and derive a little more benefit out of the 1933 season, concessionaires requested that the fair remain open past the scheduled closing date of 1 November, and the fair board granted this request, setting a new closing date of 12 November. It turned out to be a bad idea, as attendance lagged because of cold and rainy weather and, in all likelihood, the announcement that the fair would reopen in 1934. The fair board and concessions division tried their best to stimulate attendance with a number of special features. On 8 November, to celebrate the repeal of prohibition, free beer was distributed on a day ironically publicized as 'Personal Responsibility Day.' Despite 40 degree weather, 50,000 people showed up, double the previous day's crowd. They drank all the beer and ate almost 200,000 free sandwiches. Sixty people were ejected from the fairgrounds for drunkenness, although it was claimed that most of them had been drinking hard liquor from flasks. On 10 November, all persons on the relief rolls were admitted to the grounds free upon presentation of an identity card. Despite special events such as these, the fair extension did not draw enough additional visitors for most concessions to meet overhead expenses. Those that had been losing money continued to sink into the red, while those that had been profitable saw their profit margins reduced slightly.

Despite the fall in attendance during the final twelve days, many concessionaires enjoyed a successful season. Visitors spent an average of $1.12 on concessions each day. Crown Foods, with forty food stands and six restaurants, took in almost $1.7 million, and Greyhound, which provided bus transportation around the fairgrounds, earned almost $1.6 million. Sally Rand helped the Streets of Paris gross over $1.4 million, while the Sky-Ride made $757,277. Brooks Contracting Company, the pay toilet concessionaire, grossed $728,510.[5]

To help generate interest for a 1934 season, important Century of Progress exhibits were sent to various places around the country in the winter of 1933–34. Some fifty-three exhibits were taken from the fair and put on display at the McCreary & Company store in Pittsburgh, attractively displayed in settings reflecting the architecture and color of the fair. The Gutenberg workshop was sent to Philadelphia and shown at the offices of the Cuneo Eastern Press, and in Clearwater, Florida, a local World's Fair Company reconstructed the Century of Progress on a miniature scale by using building plans and photographs.[6]

There was neither the desire nor the money to make significant changes in the Century of Progress for the new season, and so visitors saw many of the same exhibits and shows that they had seen in 1933. Still, some of the changes that were made were quite evident, nowhere more so than in the color scheme. Joseph Urban had died in July 1933, and Shepard Vogelgesang had become the new Director of Color. The summer sun had badly faded some of Urban's colors, and about 75 per cent of the exterior surfaces needed to be repainted. Vogelgesang developed a new scheme, utilizing just ten colors, with no more than three, including white, on any building. At the north end of the fair, red was the dominant color, shading to red-orange by the 23rd Street entrance. Further south, at the Travel and Transport Building area, the principal color was white, with each of the major buildings using other colors for distinctive accents. The new color scheme allowed for a clearer 'zoning' principal, helping visitors find their way around by using colors as a guide, and it also meant that buildings were dominated by certain colors in a way that the more complex color scheme of the preceding year had not permitted. According to a Century of Progress guide, the new colors were designed to make the fair seem more compact, 'so the visitor won't feel like he has to walk miles and miles before he gets to the Chrysler Building from the Federal building, for example. . . . I'll bet you there will be fewer ladies complaining about sore feet this year, just on account of the colors.'[7]

Additional lighting was installed, bringing the total candlepower to 30 billion, an increase of 9 billion over 1933. This was particularly evident in and around the lagoons. Nothing had been done to provide night-time lighting in the lagoons for 1933, but for 1934, the north end of the lagoon area featured a bank of searchlights that replicated the aurora borealis, accentuated by underwater lights. A new fountain, billed as the largest in the world, was constructed 670 feet from the 12th Street bridge. It utilized 68,000 gallons of water per minute and had a 75-foot high column illuminated by five different colors of lights. Meanwhile, on dry land, 300 trees and 51,000 new flowering plants, chosen to harmonise with the new color scheme, were added, and a variety of new concessions, including restaurants and an open-air theater, were built along the edge of the lagoons.[8]

By far the most significant addition to the 1934 fair was the Ford Motor Company pavilion. Henry Ford had planned to have an exhibit at the fair in 1933, featuring an assembly line, but when General Motors announced in July 1931 that its pavilion would have an assembly line, an angry Ford said he would stay away from Chicago and hold his own exhibition. This was the Ford Exposition of Progress, a strictly automotive exhibition staged in Detroit and New York City in late 1933. Almost 3.5 million visitors flocked to see the Ford show over three and one-half weeks in the two cities. Aware that 10 million or more visitors had seen the General Motors and Chrysler pavilions at the Century of Progress in 1933, Henry Ford decided to jump in for 1934. Although Ford had never before participated in a world's fair, the Century of Progress management was thrilled to have him, and he was given an eleven-acre site near the other transportation buildings, displacing the military encampment and part of the midway. On the site, Ford erected a $2 million pavilion, designed by Albert Kahn, measuring 900 feet by 200 feet at its widest point. In the center rotunda was a 20-foot high globe showing Ford's international operations and an exhibit of sixty-seven historical automobiles. An Industrial Hall featured the latest innovations in automatic machine tools, all busily whirring and clanging and contrasting sharply with a nearby exhibit replicating Ford's original workshop where he handcrafted his first automobile. In addition, there was a bandshell in front of the pavilion where the Detroit Symphony Orchestra, sponsored by Ford, played a regular concert program for thirteen weeks, and a 2,000-foot oval walkway through a five-acre garden area between the pavilion and the lake, with nineteen sections representing different historic roadways.

Henry Ford himself took a great interest in the exhibit, personally approving such things as the style of chairs visitors could relax in and banning any sales pressure in favor of 'high-pressure good will,' despite the fact that General Motors had sold over 3,000 automobiles at its pavilion in 1933. Ford visited the site for the first time on 15 May 1934, noting that all the 'ill we have is caused by ignorance,' and asserting that a fair would help educate people and thus aid recovery by reducing ignorance. After the fair opened, Ford made thirteen visits to his pavilion and often took the time to explain the displays personally to young visitors, especially when there were newsmen and photographers nearby. The Ford exhibit received abundant praise from newspapers and trade magazines; even a Studebaker worker said, 'Ford has the most marvelous exhibit of its kind.' Visitors thought so, too; figures show that in 1934, over 75 per cent of those who came to the fair saw the Ford exhibit, compared to some 45 per cent of visitors who went to the General Motors pavilion in 1933.[9]

Other changes in 1934 were more subtle. About 75 per cent of 1933's exhibitors signed up for 1934, and with new companies, such as Ford, coming in, the total number was actually greater than in 1933. With respect to the exhibits prepared for 1934, there was more emphasis placed on live entertainment and films.

This new attention to entertainment worked even in the staid Hall of Science. Visitors were more interested in seeing people (or people-like machines) do something or appear to do something. Dr Carey Croneis, a geologist charged with reviewing the pure science exhibits for 1934, subjected each to a three-question test: 1) Is it simple?; 2) Can it relate to some common experience of the visitor?; 3) Does it move? New exhibits which met these guidelines included apparatus for detecting cosmic rays, a staple at many later expositions, and an exhibit on 'heavy' water. Popular exhibits from the year before, such as the Transparent Man, were given more space, and other exhibits were made more lively.

Commercial exhibitors were able to refine their presentations to keep the good from 1933 and alter the bad. Chrysler, for example, made much more use of its quarter-mile testing track, adding a grandstand and sponsoring stock car races. Standard Oil Company discarded its films about the petroleum industry in favor of a free wild animal act that told visitors nothing about oil but kept the company name in front of them. The Studebaker theater, built in the shape of a large car, climaxed its presentation with a descent into a rock quarry, while Hupmobile brought in a test-driving film that simulated real driving conditions. Visitors who completed the test drive were given a certificate. The Safety Glass Company dared visitors to break a window by throwing rocks at it. Armour, the meat-packing company, had a popular bacon slicing and wrapping demonstration, employing 'auburn-haired beauties' to run the machines. General Electric showed off its modern appliances and offered one-hour cooking courses, while the Flexible Shaft Company, which made the 'Mixmaster,' utilized 'pretty girl' demonstrators to show the uses of the machine. An 'expansive' Aunt Jemima flipped pancakes for Quaker Oats, and Libby, McNeill and Libby employed 'smartly-uniformed girls' to pack Spanish olives 'artistically' in glass jars. Even Petrolagar, a laxative, succeeded with a realistic diorama based on a famous painting of a doctor treating a sick child while his parents stood by.[10]

In the Housing exhibit, George Fred Keck replaced his House of Tomorrow with the 'Crystal House.' This experimental glass and steel house was designed to be an ultra-modern, low-cost single family residence that could be erected quickly. Its plate glass walls and steel framing members were prefabricated and assembled on a concrete slab poured at the site. A central utility core contained mechanical equipment, and sliding draperies afforded privacy. Because of the glass walls, a sophisticated heating and cooling system was required, and while the house did have a rather dramatic appearance, its significance was more as a symbol of modernism than as a practical prototype for residential housing.

Apart from Keck's work, only minor changes were made in the Housing exhibit, although the Stran-Steel company built a smaller 'subsistence' house on its lot that left room for the construction of a 'skeleton' version to show visitors how the house was built. Stran-Steel also placed a man with a microphone outside the house, with the sound piped in so that a dialogue could be carried on with a tour guide in such a way that it seemed as if the steel frame of the house were talking. In July, the fair sponsored 'A Century of Progress Better Housing Forum,' to which representatives of more the 500 women's groups were invited. The program consisted of discussions concerning local, state, and federal housing programs and a number of prominent speakers, including Coleman Woodbury, chairman of the Illinois Housing Commission, who spoke on 'Why Low Cost Housing?' On Home Modernization Day, 24 October, a century-old house that had been moved from the city to the area of the housing exhibit was completely remodeled by volunteer workers in one day at an estimated materials cost of between $750 and $1,000.[11]

Congress appropriated $175,000 to alter or refurbish federal government exhibits, but little was actually changed for 1934. The Federal Building needed repairs to its roof and reflecting pool and was repainted white with red and orange trim. Because of the new Ford pavilion, the military encampment, renamed Camp Franklin D. Roosevelt, was moved to a smaller site on Northerly Island near the Federal Building. The cavalry and most of the artillery did not return, but there were larger contingents of naval and marine personnel. Under the new US commissioner, eighty-year-old former Illinois governor E. F. Dunne, and Assistant Commissioner Causey, most of the other agencies made only minor changes in their exhibits and concerned themselves with post-fair planning, although a special three-day exhibit of the work of the Civilian Conservation Corps in October attracted 28,000 visitors and much favorable comment and demand for the craft items produced by the workers.[12]

The Hall of Science was again one of the most popular buildings, with its displays of basic scientific and mathematical principles. Improvements were made in the way exhibits were dramatized; many were simplified. The interdependence of scientific fields was emphasized in such displays as the giant periodic table of the elements, a 'Clock of the Ages,' showing the geological history of the earth in forty-two seconds, and a large model of a molecule of sodium chloride, or simple table salt. The number of medical exhibits, which had proven very popular in 1933, was increased by 50 per cent.[13]

The effects of the depression, however, limited official or semi-official participation in 1934 to just six foreign governments and eleven state governments. An effort was made to attract more foreign participation by turning the Hall of States into a Court of Nations and offering space there to foreign governments, but it was unsuccessful. Only Greece mounted an exhibit in the Hall of States, although some vacant space was occupied by the Chicago Park system, the city of Chicago, and the Virgin Islands. Some blame for the decrease in foreign participation was placed on the 1928 Paris convention, as the extension of the Century of Progress was deemed to be a violation of that agreement. Sweden and Czechoslovakia, as a result, changed their participation from official to semi-official. Another problem may have been caused by the fact that the Illinois legislature did not officially permit the continued use of the site until 22 February 1934, which may have prohibited new participants from coming to Chicago because of the lack of preparation time. In the end, China, Italy, and Spain had official exhibits, while Sweden, Czechoslovakia, and Greece were represented semi-officially. Many states communicated to the fair management that their legislatures simply could not appropriate the funds necessary to continue on in 1934, and several, including California, Colorado, and Georgia, that did exhibit in 1934 were unable to pay their bills to the fair.[14]

Because of the notoriety of Sally Rand's fan dancing and other acts involving nudity, there had been some sharp criticism of the 'nasty and vulgar features' of the Century of Progress midway. Walter R. Mee, speaking on behalf of the Committee for a Century of Progress through Religion, demanded in October 1933 that peep shows and other 'salacious' exhibits be kept out of the 1934 fair; if not, all participation by religious groups would be withdrawn. Since the religious exhibits had ranked just behind those in the Hall of Science in popularity, the fair management took the demand seriously, admitted that the Midway for 1933 was 'far from satisfactory' (although the Belgian Village had been very well received), and promised to clean up the shows. It was clear that visitors would continue to demand midway entertainment, but because of the new Ford pavilion, a large part of the Midway was moved to a more obscure location on the lakefront behind the Agricultural Building and the Federal and States group. The fair staff also pledged to control concessionaires more closely, continue the censoring of nudity, and crack down on outside hawking and blaring loudspeakers.

At first, it looked as if the Century of Progress was serious about censoring shows of questionable morality. On 1 June 1934, just a few days after the second season opened, Nathaniel Owings, the new chief of concessions, shut down the popular Streets of Paris concession because of two objectionable shows – Olympia and Visions of Art – both of which featured nearly nude models posing in artistically lighted sets. The concessionaire, John MacMahon, promised to change the shows, and Streets of Paris reopened the next day, but MacMahon defended his shows: 'We thought the Fair was dead and just tried to pep it up. . . . We thought we were showing art.'

A week later, a compromise on nude dancing between the concessionaire's association and Owings' office was announced. All parties agreed that 'common sense and decency' should prevail, and while some enforcement against nude shows continued (three shows were shut down at the Italian Village the very next day), much less was heard about the problem.

The most significant change in the entertainment side of the fair was the addition of many new villages, whose investors and managers hoped to duplicate the 1933 success of the Belgian Village and the Streets of Paris. Under the leadership of Owings, fifteen villages were in the fold by May 1934, far too many for traffic to bear. Consequently, many, such as the Irish Village and the Spanish Village, failed, although the Black Forest Village, which featured daily ice skating shows, was a major success. Despite efforts on the part of the fair board to ameliorate the financial crises of some of the villages, such as deferring the collection of money owed or lending them money on the condition they would stay open at least through Labor Day, most of the villages were losing propositions in 1934; it was estimated that investors in these villages collectively lost some $2 million.[15]

The contract with the Art Institute was renewed for the 1934 season, and that year, the theme was 'American Art,' viewed in the context of world art. The exhibit, said to be valued at $75 million, showed more than 350 masterpieces borrowed from Europe, including works by El Greco and Rembrandt and a large display of French impressionism, set off against a like number of American paintings from colonial times to the 1930s. The exhibit paid special attention to the work of James A. McNeill Whistler, whose birth centennial was being commemorated, as well as Thomas Eakins and Winslow Homer, considered among the greatest of nineteenth century American painters. The most popular painting, however, was *Execution of Edith Cavell*, by George Bellows, which the *Chicago Tribune* critic labeled the 'sensation' picture of the exhibit.[16]

On 31 May 1934, just a few days after the season opened, over 500,000 visitors braved 98 degree heat to attend the fair on Children's Day, with children admitted for five cents and given a free bottle of milk at the entrance gate. This attendance was higher than any day during the 1933 season and encouraged the management to declare that on every Thursday children would be admitted for a nickel. Although there were no serious accidents, fair officials reported that 200 visitors were treated for sunburn and other heat-related ailments and 1,400 children were lost for varying lengths of time.

Toward the end of the 1934 season, the management set aside two days for families on relief to see the fair without charge. This gesture, which had been done the year before, pleased Mayor Kelly, who said, '[I]t has been my fond hope that no man, woman, or child living in Cook County should be denied the opportunity of seeing [the fair] before it closes forever on October 31.' Some 51,000 came.[17]

Chicago's great world's fairs

The final day of the Century of Progress, 31 October 1934, attracted 195,577 visitors, many of them city employees who came after Mayor Kelly declared a half holiday at noon; many businesses and schools also closed. At closing time, there was a rush to scavenge movable items as 'souvenirs' of the fair, but police made most people leave their items inside the gates. Only one man was arrested; he had wrapped a toilet seat in an American flag and was booked for disrespect to the flag and fined $25. The damage caused on the last day amounted to only about $5,000, since much of what the public pulled down or apart was to be demolished anyway.

With a 1934 attendance of 16,486,377 (including 171,897 tickets bought but not used), fair management ended the season with a surplus of $688,165 to cover the costs of demolition, organizational expenses, future claims, and any contingencies. The receipts in the final weeks enabled the board to make a final disbursement of $587,500 to bondholders; the Century of Progress was the only world's fair to pay off bondholders in full. Despite the woes of some of the village concessionaires, fair managers were quite satisfied with the overall success of the 1934 season. Fairgoers spent just over $1 each on concessions, down only slightly from 1933. Greyhound, whose buses took visitors around the site, grossed $812,344; Crown Foods, with its forty-seven food stands and nine restaurants, earned almost $1.3 million; the Sky-Ride took in $345,255; Wings of a Century, $220,568; Midget City, $195,542; and Streets of Paris, $182,555. Even the 'Guess Your Weight' machines earned $182,663. Many concessionaires expressed their willingness to stay a third year, and others made plans to participate in future world's fairs or other amusement venues. The Streets of Paris, for example, took its structure and subconcessionaires and went to Miami for the winter season.[18]

The city of Chicago continued to derive economic benefit from the Century of Progress in 1934. A 31 October *Chicago Tribune* article pointed out that the fair had generated an estimated 50,000 temporary or permanent jobs during its two years and had brought about $50 million of construction and maintenance work. Out-of-town visitors had left $700 million in the pockets of the Chicago business community, part of which had gone to increase local and state tax receipt by a cumulative $54 million over the 1932 total. The economic boom had also resulted in a decrease of 68 per cent in unmet payrolls and other obligations during the run of the fair. Hotel business had been excellent at all levels of accommodation, and the fair had provided a notable cultural uplift to the city; some 34 million people had passed through the Hall of Science. Mindful of this, the Chicago city council passed a resolution on 8 November authorizing the appointment of a committee to look into ways in which the Century of Progress could be maintained as a permanent exposition in Chicago. The resolution, supported by Mayor Kelly, requested the state to pass the necessary legislation for the continued use of the land and assigned the committee the task of raising $2.5 million to reopen the fair on a sound financial footing. The *Chicago Tribune* also argued for the continuance of the fair, or some similar kind of show. Estimating that 40,000 people in Chicago owed their current employment to the Century of Progress, the newspaper hoped they could keep their jobs in connection with a continuing educational and entertaining activity. Without such a continuation, the 5,000 Century of Progress employees would surely be out of a job when the fair closed, and many others would find their livelihood endangered. By this time, however, there was scant interest among the fair management to continue on with their arduous task. They had achieved their goal of putting on a splendid show and repaying those who had placed financial trust in them, and the desire to go on just for the sake of going on was not there; 'the orange had been squeezed dry.' As quickly as it could, the fair board moved ahead with the process of liquidation and demolition.[19]

Notes

1 Franklin D. Roosevelt, quoted in the *Chicago Tribune*, 22 October 1933.
2 Franklin D. Roosevelt to Rufus Dawes, 11 October 1933, COP 9–133; J. C. Folsom to Carl Strand, 26 October 1933, COP 1–14190; *Chicago Tribune*, 4 November 1933.
3 Frank B. Jewett to Rufus Dawes, 6 November 1933, COP 5–253; Dawes to Jewett, 9 November 1933, COP 5–253.
4 'A Century of Progress paradox,' *Architectural Forum*, LXI, November 1934, pp. 378–79; Press Releases, COP, 5 January 1934 and 15 January 1934, COP Papers, RG 43, Entry 1392, Box 12, National Archives.
5 A. N. Gonsior, 'Report of the special features division,' p. 14, COP 15–102; *Chicago Tribune*, 1, 3, 7 and 9 November 1933. Until 1 November, the average daily attendance had been 127,430. From 1 November until the fair closed on 12 November, the average daily attendance was only 51,715. Even on closing day, only 92,262 attended.
6 Century of Progress, *Progress*, 1, 15 January 1934, p. 4.
7 *Chicago Tribune*, 17, 22, 23 and 26 May 1934.
8 Lenox R. Lohr, *Fair Management: The Story of a Century of Progress Exposition*, Chicago, 1952, pp. 79–80; Louis Skidmore, Memorandum on exterior color scheme for 1934, 10 March 1934, COP 5–27; 'A Century of Progress, 1934,' World's Fair Supplement, *Chicago International Market*, 1934, pp. 8, 36.
9 'A Century of Progress, 1934,' p. 10; J. Parker Van Zandt and L. Rohe Walter, 'King customer at a Century of Progress,' *Review of Reviews*, XC, September 1934,

pp. 22–27; 'Ford exposition at Chicago,' *Literary Digest*, CXVII, 18 August 1934, p. 6; David L. Lewis, *The Public Image of Henry Ford*, Detroit, 1976, pp. 298–301; 'Welding in the Ford building at the 1934 Century of Progress,' *Architectural Record*, LXXV, June 1934, p. 467; *Chicago Tribune*, 16 May 1934.

10   Van Zandt and Walter, 'King customer,' pp. 22–27; Rufus C. Dawes, 'A Century of Progress adds a year,' *Literary Digest*, CXVII, 9 June 1934, p. 32; 'A Century of Progress, 1934,' p. 35; *Chicago Tribune*, 23 May 1934.

11   Thomas M. Slade, 'The "Crystal House" of 1934,' *Journal of the Society of Architectural Historians*, XXIX, December 1970, pp. 350–53; Press Releases, COP, 9 July, 22 October, 23 October 1934, COP 14–161; F. C. Boggs to Secretary, 13 April 1934, COP 1–14190; E. O. Brady to Folsom, 15 May 1934, COP 1–14190; Brady to Chester H. Walcott, 4 June 1934, COP 1–14190; Final report 1934, COP Papers, RG 43, Entry 1392, Box 6, National Archives.

12   'Science at the Century of Progress exposition in 1934,' *Scientific Monthly*, XXXIX, November 1934, pp. 475–78; Final report 1934, COP Papers, RG 43, Entry 1392, Box 6, National Archives; 'Report on special activities,' COP Papers, RG 43, Entry 1392, Box 6, National Archives.

13   'A Century of Progress, 1934,' pp. 32–34.

14   Press release, COP, 5 January 1934, COP Papers, RG 43, Entry 1392, Box 12, National Archives; Final Report 1934, COP Papers, RG 43, Entry 1392, Box 6, National Archives.

15   F. C. Boggs to Causey, 13 February 1934, COP Papers, RG 43, Entry 1392, Box 9, National Archives; Charles T. Holman, 'Chicago fair to reopen in 1934,' *Christian Century*, L, 29 November 1933, p. 1513; Minutes of executive committee, COP, 9 August 1934, COP 5–120; 'A Century of Progress, 1934,' pp. 31–32; Press release, COP, 23 December 1933, COP Papers, RG 43, Entry 1392, Box 12, National Archives; *Chicago Tribune*, 26 October 1933, 2 and 8 June 1934; 'A Century of Progress paradox,' pp. 376–78. Lawyers for the Century of Progress advised the board of trustees that the fair could lend money to failing concessions only if by not doing so, the entire fair would be damaged by the forced closing of an important feature.

16   *Chicago Tribune*, 26 and 31 May 1934. A very thorough description of the exhibition, including a list of the paintings included, is in 'Art of America is feature of Chicago's great 1934 exhibition,' *Art Digest*, VIII, June 1934, pp. 5–24.

17   *Chicago Tribune*, 20 May, 24 May and 1 June 1934; Press Release, COP, 15 October 1934, BBC, Box 16, Folder 5.

18   *Chicago Tribune*, 21, 23 and 31 October, 1 and 9 November 1934; Cathy Cahan and Richard Cahan, 'The lost city of the depression,' *Chicago History, IV*, Winter 1976–77, pp. 238–40.

19   *Chicago Tribune*, 21 October and 13 November 1934; 'Chicago fair: exposition ends with riots and profits,' *Newsweek, IV*, 10 November 1934, p. 32.

11   Postscript to the fair

> We think the Fair is wonderful and we have a great deal to see and hope to get up there several times before fall. . . . As a young boy, I joined a military company to be able to go to the 1893 World's Fair and I naturally thought that I would never see as nice a Fair again but for color and beauty this one is the winner.[1]

Three major elements comprised the dismantling of the Century of Progress Exposition. First, beginning very soon after the fair closed, there was a series of sealed bid auctions to dispose of the furniture, fixtures, and other portable assets on the grounds. Second, there was the process of demolishing the many buildings and other structures on the site and returning the land to its pre-fair condition. And third, there was the final accounting for the fair, which involved settling remaining debts and disbursing the surplus according to a pre-arranged formula.

A series of several sealed bid auctions were held beginning 12 November 1934. Bidders could submit bids by mail, enclosing a percentage of the total of their bids as a deposit. Several such sales were conducted between November and the following March, which netted about $80,000. Although the major purchasers of goods were commercial salvage companies which bought large quantities of light fixtures, office furniture, mechanical equipment, and janitorial supplies, some individuals picked up outstanding bargains. C. B. Hobson of Chicago bought the Pinto Brothers Motor Boat ride with a capacity of eighteen 'kiddies' for $70, H. E. Skinner of Chicago bought a 1929 Lincoln seven-passenger 'limousine' for $127.50, sculptor John Storrs reclaimed four bas-reliefs he had done for the lobby of the Trustee's Lounge for $12, J. B. Wolfson of Cincinnati bought thirty-three used 24-inch floor squeegees for $3.33, and Lenox Lohr bought an 18-foot fishing boat for $26.10 and a 36-inch band saw for $21.[2]

Although DePauw University in Greencastle, Indiana, bought ten historical dioramas for $6, very few of the fair's exhibits were sold. Most went back to the university, corporation, or government agency that had provided them, while much material, particularly from the federal government exhibits, was given or loaned to the Museum of Science and Industry. The government also earned $440.75 from the sale at auction of a few surplus items.[3]

Individual concessionaires who had built their own structures were obligated to demolish them, but a number of them paid the Century of Progress varying sums to be released from that obligation. In January 1935, a Springfield, Illinois, contractor agreed to pay $28,000 to carry out the demolition, keeping whatever materials he could salvage. But in July, with much still to be removed, the fair board signed an agreement with the Chicago Park District (formerly the South Park Commission) in which the fair paid the park district $125,000 in cash and $150,000 in Chicago River Bridge and Approach bonds to release the Century of Progress from its obligation to demolish a long list of fair buildings and other structures, including the Agricultural Building, the Hall of States, the Electrical Group, the Hall of Science, the General Exhibits Building, the Travel and Transport Building, the Home Planning Hall, the Sky-Ride, and the stage for the Wings of a Century pageant. Most of this work was carried out over the next few months by contractors engaged by the park district.[4]

A few structures survived past the original demolition program. The fair's Administration Building, the first structure to be built on the site, was used as a park district headquarters until 1940, when it was razed. Fort Dearborn was left as a tourist attraction, but the costs of maintenance proved too great, and it was torn down after it partially burned in 1939. The Golden Temple of Jehol was dismantled by Works Progress Administration workers in 1938 and sent to the New York World's Fair, which opened the following year. Six of the homes from the housing exhibit, including the Rostone House, were moved and re-erected at Beverly Shores, Indiana, by developer Robert Bartlett, and two others were moved to residential neighborhoods in Chicago. The rotunda and part of one wing of the Ford pavilion were moved to a site near Ford's River Rouge plant in Michigan. Rebuilt with limestone walls and opened in May 1936, the structure contained a display area for new automobile models, an exhibition hall, and a theater. The Terrazzo Promenade, a mosaic walkway in front of the Adler Planetarium, was destroyed in 1971, when the planetarium underwent an expansion.[5]

It was not until December 1937 that the board wound up its financial affairs by setting aside up to $7,000 for the writing and publication of a history of the Century of Progress and then authorizing the disbursement of surplus funds. During the three years following the fair's closing in 1934, bad debts had been scrutinized and a total of about $93,000 written off, principally from proprietors of failed villages during the 1934 season. The demolition and return of the grounds to the Chicago Park District had been concluded in February 1936, and settlements of suits with the city over water usage during the fair and with a title company that had been the depository for fair bonds had been reached. The surplus that remained, $160,000, was distributed according to a formula made before the fair opened: the Park District and the Museum of Science and Industry each received 25 per cent; the Art Institute received 20 per cent; the Adler Planetarium received 10 per cent; the Archeological Trust of Chicago and the Fort Dearborn trust each received 5 per cent; the Chicago Regional Plan received 4 per cent; and the Yerkes Observatory and the Smithsonian Institution each received 3 per cent.[6]

The people involved with the Century of Progress soon went their own way, although the board of trustees remained intact until the accounts were settled in 1937. Rufus Dawes became head of the Museum of Science and Industry and served in that capacity until his death in 1940. Lenox Lohr went to New York as president of the National Broadcasting System, taking Martha McGrew along with him; upon Dawes's death, he returned to Chicago and assumed Dawes's post at the museum, remaining there until his death in 1968. C. S. Peterson accepted the post of honorary president of the Golden Gate International Exposition in San Francisco in 1939–40, J. Franklin Bell was its executive vice-president, and Shepard Vogelgesang worked as the director of decorative arts. Louis Skidmore and Nathaniel Owings became partners in Skidmore, Owings and Merrill, the largest architectural and commercial design firm in the United States for many years after World War II. Charles G. Dawes returned in 1932 from his ambassadorship in Britain to direct the Reconstruction Finance Corporation in the Hoover administration. Forrest Moulton returned to academic life, writing books and serving for many years as administrative secretary of the American Academy for the Advancement of Science. Otto Teegen was color director at the Great Lakes Exposition in Cleveland in 1936, and the co-ordinating architect for the Town of Tomorrow attraction at the New York World's Fair, 1939–40. Allen D. Albert spent a number of years as director of an art gallery in Terre Haute, Indiana. Among the architects, most retired or returned to private practice, although Arthur Brown served as chairman of the architectural board for the Golden

Gate International Exposition, and Ralph Walker designed several buildings for the New York World's Fair.

In November 1934, A Century of Progress Re-employment Association, an organization to try and find new jobs for former fair workers, was formed. Although the association was not funded by the Century of Progress, it was successful in placing 367 former employees in new jobs, about fifty of which were permanent positions. Unfortunately, the organization had no money with which to operate, and a $250 donation from the fair board in January 1935 kept it going only a short while longer.[7]

Silas Fung and Edna Bobsin were two Chicagoans for whom the fair had a special significance. While probably not typical of all fairgoers, the stories of Fung and Bobsin tell us what kind of an impact such a fair can have on the people who visit it.

Silas Fung was born in Shanghai and came to the United States in 1921. After living for two years on the west coast, he moved to Chicago in 1923, where he worked as a freelance commercial artist and was active in the Chinese community. Using a season pass obtained from the Chinese consul, Fung went to the fair virtually every week in 1933 and 1934, spending most of his time in the Hall of Science and the General Exhibits building, and frequently having lunch at the restaurant that was a part of the Chinese village behind the Hall of Science. He loved the colors and the 'futuristic' architecture and thought that the fair would become a permanent attraction in Chicago.

The more he saw of the fair, Fung said in an interview, the more sentimental he felt about it, and when it was over and about to be razed, he had an urge to collect pieces of it before they were gone. He acquired a pass to visit the site during the demolition period and over a period of some months collected a small piece of each of forty-two Century of Progress buildings, which he kept in the basement storage room of his apartment building. When his landlady threatened to throw his relics away, he designed a model building in a composite of the fair's architectural style and had a professional model builder construct it for him.

Fung continued to collect other items from the fair and built a kind of shrine to it in his apartment, attracting visits at various times from Rufus Dawes, Lenox Lohr, and Martha McGrew. He organized a tenth anniversary celebration in 1944, which Lohr attended. In 1952, he and his wife moved to Haines City, Florida, and in the late 1950s, he converted a small house into a museum for the Century of Progress. There he displayed his model building, as well as a large number of other authentic items from the Century of Progress and the many subsequent fairs he attended. In addition, he built a projection booth into his museum and showed the official film of the fair. By 1984, some 4,000 had visited his World's Fairama in Haines City. In 1992, at the age of eighty-nine, Fung donated his collection to Chicago's Museum of Science and Industry, where it was dedicated in a ceremony commemorating the centennial of the World's Columbian Exposition.[8]

Edna Bobsin was a young woman from Chicago who attended the fair some thirty-one times over its two seasons. Although we know nothing of her personal life, we know this because of the elaborately detailed scrapbook she made to remember her experiences at the fair. Bobsin's scrapbook, well over 100 pages, contains hundreds of postcards, newspaper photographs, and fair souvenirs, all meticulously arranged and annotated. The opening pages of her scrapbook contain pictures and references to the World's Columbian Exposition and general information about the Century of Progress. Later pages then proceed logically through the fairgrounds, carefully and usually dispassionately chronicling each building and its exhibits in considerable detail. The latter half of the scrapbook recounts her 1934 visits and carefully notes what was different about the fair in its second year.

Although much of Bobsin's commentary is straightforward and purely descriptive, we can learn from occasional remarks what it was at the fair that she particularly enjoyed. She liked the exhibits in the Hall of Science, especially the Transparent Man, and the diorama based on the painting, *The Doctor*, and she was impressed by the 'marvelous' murals depicting the steel industry in the General Exhibits Building. Although she twice referred to the automobiles being produced in the General Motors pavilion as Chryslers, she thought the assembly line was noteworthy. The Norwegian windjammer, *Sorlandet*, was 'a most beautiful sight' with its sails unfurled, and Wings of a Century was 'well worth [the] price.' Detailed descriptions of the exhibits in the Travel and Transportation Building and of the Wonder Bread baking exhibit testify to her interest in those areas, and, although she does not record having seen Sally Rand's dance, she thought that the Holland Dutch Village (sic) was one of the 'most quaint and interesting as well as one of the most colorful of the 1934 villages.' She particularly liked the Standard Oil Live Power Show, a circus-like animal act, featuring 'many lions, tigers, and lepers (sic).' If there were features she did not care for, she did not include them in her scrapbook, for there are virtually no negative comments.

For each season of the fair, Bobsin listed the days she went and who, if anyone, accompanied her. Of her thirty-one visits, about ten were by herself, a few were with her parents, and the others were with various female friends or married couples. She followed the fair through its demolition phase; the last picture in the scrapbook is a news photo of the collapse of the east Sky-Ride tower on 29 August 1935.

Unfortunately, there is no record of the post-fair life of Edna Bobsin, where she lived and worked, whether she married and had children, when she died. But the fact that the scrapbook was so carefully created and arranged, and preserved in excellent condition for well over fifty years after the fair, suggests that the fair was a very important part of her life.[9]

Articles published in the *Chicago Tribune* in commemoration of the fortieth and fiftieth anniversaries of the fair reveal the lingering fond memories many visitors retained. When a fortieth reunion gala was scheduled for former fair employees in 1973, organizers received many requests for invitations. Others spoke of the escape the Century of Progress provided from the depression: 'It seemed as if one could flee the Depression simply by plunking down 50 cents and walking thru (sic) the gate.' Some recognized the benefit of the fair to Chicago: 'It was a tremendous shot in the arm for everyone concerned, . . . and it's the reason why Chicago became known as a 'fair' town from that time forward.'[10]

As with the World's Columbian Exposition, the Century of Progress is remembered in a tangible way by the multitude of souvenirs and mementoes it produced. The US Post Office issued two stamps, both as single stamps and in souvenir sheets of twenty-five, and the postal station at the site had special cancellations of various kinds. Probably no other fair had the amount and variety of picture postcards as did the Century of Progress; perhaps as many as 200 manufacturers printed single cards for a particular exhibitor or lengthy series of cards showing views of the fair. Several different pictorial view books were published, in addition to the official guidebook, and most of the exhibitors distributed a pamphlet, brochure, or leaflet extolling their product line. Souvenir shops both inside and outside the fairgrounds were full of a wide variety of three-dimensional mementoes of the fair. There were pot metal ashtrays, silver-plated tie clasps, copper good luck tokens, felt pennants, and silk scarves, most bearing the logo of the exposition. Paper collectables, such as beer coasters, decks of cards, and official certificates of attendance, found their way into the scrapbooks of many visitors. Maurice L. Rothschild, a haberdasher in the Loop, offered for one dollar a Century of Progress necktie in seven colors with a design showing the architectural style of fair buildings. Sears, Roebuck & Company sponsored a national quilt contest, with a first prize of $1,200, that attracted some 25,000 entries, many of which incorporated design features from the fair into their work and are significant collectables today. These and many other tokens sustained the affectionate memories that so many visitors had of this fair, and they provide contemporary students with a material link to the event.[11]

There was almost a third Chicago world's fair, and perhaps if the promoters had studied the history of the first two more thoroughly, the projected 1992 fair might have occurred. In 1977, Chicago architect Harry Weese suggested a world's fair to celebrate the quincentennial of Columbus's discovery of the New World and incidentally, the centennial of the World's Columbian Exposition. The idea attracted other prominent Chicagoans, including Thomas G. Ayers, a utility company executive, and in 1981, the Chicago World's Fair-1992 Corporation was formed, with Ayers as its president. This corporation, which consisted of influential corporate leaders, lawyers, and architects, worked for several months without public or political input and planned the theme, site, and dates for a 1992 fair and prepared an application for obtaining the sanction of the Bureau international des expositions (BIE). The site selected was roughly the same as that for the Century of Progress Exposition, centered at Burnham Harbor, though shifted several blocks to the north.

By 1982, the closed nature of the fair corporation's decision-making process and the feeling that important issues were being ignored began to generate opposition to the fair. Much of the criticism revolved around the perilous financing of the fair, the environmental impact, and the effect that the fair would have on nearby residential neighborhoods. Late in the year, state and city officials combined to create a formal Chicago World's Fair-1992 Authority to replace the secretive Fair corporation, while assorted opponents of the event coalesced into the Chicago 1992 Committee.

The election of Harold Washington as mayor in April 1983 was significant to the proposed 1992 fair since, unlike his predecessor, Jane Byrne, he was rather skeptical about the fair. Criticism, both in and out of the Washington administration, revolved around the amount of public spending necessary for such things as altering major roadways in the vicinity of the site, building sewers, and providing police and fire protection for the fair. Others questioned the reality of the Fair Authority's attendance and economic projections, and, more ominously, whether the leadership of the pro-fair forces was using the fair to boost land values in nearby areas in which they had financial interests.

Further debate continued through 1984 and into 1985, and chances for the fair dimmed further when news of the financial debacle of the 1984 New Orleans fair was publicized. The final blow, however, came in June 1985, when a feasibility study commissioned by Michael Madigan, the speaker of the Illinois House of Representatives, concluded that the proposed fair was such a bad financial risk that it should not be underwritten with state money. Without state funds, the fair could not be staged, and although some proponents of the event clung to the hope of mounting a smaller, privately-financed event, public support was virtually non-existent, and in December 1987, the BIE withdrew its sanction for the Chicago fair.[12]

The 1992 fair for Chicago was killed by the fear that it would become a $300 million financial disaster for the city. Critics railed the fair proponents for their lack of sound business and financial sense, among other things, saying that the projections of attendance, income, and expenditures were nothing more than wishful thinking and did not reflect sound business sense. The travail of the 1992 fair contrasts nicely with an important feature of the Century of Progress. Above all, the Century of Progress was a business proposition. Throughout the planning, operation, and aftermath of the exposition, Dawes, Lohr, and their lieutenants were acutely aware of the financial status of their project. The fact that the fair managers, working in the midst of a global economic crisis of immense proportions, accepted no government subsidies, paid off their investors in full, and ended with a surplus of $160,000 was a matter of immense pride to them. To many, the profit that was earned may have brought more satisfaction than the quality of the show they put on. Most of the Century of Progress managers were corporate business leaders, and profits were their *raison d'être*.

The leaders of the World's Columbian Exposition, on the other hand, were businesspeople as well, to be sure, but more than that, they were the social and cultural elite of 1890s Chicago, men who had a great stake in their city and wanted to create an image of Chicago and its people that suited their notion of what an ideal city should be. Chicago as a city had much to be proud of in 1893. It had made a remarkable recovery from the fire of 1871, it had grown fivefold in the years since the fire, and it had become the center of the nation's rail system and the focus of American commercial architecture during those years. But the World's Columbian

Exposition turned its back on the real city and created an illusory city, with illusory architecture, and buildings constructed of illusory marble. And, as we have seen, it was a successful illusion. Visitors were awe-struck by the classical forms of the buildings, the formality of the Court of Honor, and the whiteness of it all. They were tantalized and titillated by the sights and sounds (and probably the odors, as well) of the Midway, and they were at least intrigued with the massive number of industrial, agricultural, and historical exhibits. For these reasons, the World's Columbian Exposition was an important and influential event, not just in the history of fairs, where its influence is unquestioned, but also in the development of commercial architecture, city planning, department stores, museums, and urban entertainment forms, such as the amusement park.

Although it shared a host city with the World's Columbian Exposition and even shared the experience of operating during an economic depression, the Century of Progress could hardly have been more different. The Columbian Exposition was spread out over half again as many acres as the Century of Progress; there one could actually get away from the crowds and walk in green parkland. At the Century of Progress, the mood was more intense, and at every turn, visitors encountered a dramatic new building or fairground 'gadget.' While visitors were, for the most part, impressed with the dramatic forms and colors of the buildings at the Century of Progress, one would be hard pressed to say they were awe-struck by them, and indeed, more than a few found the cacophony of colors and angles difficult to appreciate. Still, the architecture of the fair helped to popularize a kind of streamlined Art Deco style that found fuller flowering five years later at the New York World's Fair.

Although both fairs stressed science, technology, and progress in their exhibitry, each approached the matter of exhibiting in a distinctive way. In order to show the state of progress up to 1893, the World's Columbian Exposition used the department store method, wherein static exhibits of industrial products were lined up on shelves or placed in display cases, just as they might have been in a retail store. Companies competed with one another for the prizes that were awarded to those products judged the finest, and there was a good deal of nationalistic pride in seeing that American goods had been judged superior to foreign products.

Prizes were not awarded at the Century of Progress, and at this fair, the emphasis was on process rather than product. While the fair's planners certainly wanted to celebrate a century of scientific and technological progress, they also wanted to show 'how good things grow out of science' and suggest that the future holds much better things for Americans through the miracles wrought by science and technology. If the Columbian Exposition was a department store, then the Century of Progress was a school laboratory. The best exhibits were those that moved in some purposeful way, or made a product as visitors watched, or used visual or animated aids to tell a story; at their extreme, the exhibits seemed to show that 'modern scientific practice is a combination of Hollywood and Houdini.' Even the fair-sponsored Midway or entertainment events, such as The World a Million Years Ago and Wings of a Century, tried to teach a lesson. Indeed, the emphasis on teaching and learning was so great that some critics expressed the opinion that the fair tried to be too didactic and was not sufficiently entertaining in a mindless way. Bruce Bliven attributed this to the fundamental character of midwesterners: 'The perfect characterization of these worthy people is to be found in the fact that the popcorn sold at the Fair is accompanied by a chemical analysis, printed on the box, which proves that it is highly nourishing. No good Middle Westerner would eat popcorn just for fun.'[13]

The Century of Progress Exposition was at once an escape from the trials of the depression, an adult education center, a successful business venture, and a contributor to the development of modernist architecture. That it has not been studied more follows from the scholarly eclipse all fairs have been shadowed by until relatively recently, the sense that it was a *Chicago* fair with little significance outside that city, and the flippancy that many historians of architecture and design have seen in its buildings, colors, and exhibits.

All that is history's loss. The Century of Progress was, on the whole, a good fair that met the challenge of its times with distinctive architecture, sound business management, and an important educational objective. It worked well as a small city within a city, and the vast majority of visitors were very pleased with what they experienced. It served as an important model for subsequent fairs in San Diego in 1935 and New York and San Francisco in 1939–40. And had the city of Chicago gone ahead with its plans to hold a world's fair in 1992 for the quincentennial of Columbus's discovery of America, the Century of Progress would have been there, in documentary records and fading memory, to lend a helping hand.

Notes

1 W. B. Causey to E. Ross Bartley, 20 July 1933, quoting from letter of Hugh H. Bolton to Harry S. New, Century of Progress Papers, RG 43, Entry 1392, Box 12, National Archives.

2 Records of salvage sales, COP 10–12022–23, 10–12026; Lenox R. Lohr, *Fair Management: The Story of a Century of Progress Exposition*, Chicago, 1952, pp. 264–65.

3 O. T. Kreusser to Lt. Col. Dan I. Sultan, 29 August 1933, Century of Progress Papers, RG 43, Entry 1392, Box 9, National Archives; Final Report 1934, Century of Progress Papers, RG 43, Entry 1392, Box 6, National Archives.

4 Resolution, Executive Committee, 3 July 1935, COP 5–117; Minutes of meeting of executive committee, 3 January 1935, COP 5–119; Lohr, *Fair Management*, p. 264.

5 *Chicago Tribune*, 3 June 1973; David L. Lewis, *The Public Image of Henry Ford*, Detroit, 1976, p. 301; Cathy Cahan and Richard Cahan, 'The lost city of the depression,' *Chicago History*, IV, Winter 1976–77, pp. 241–42; Lohr, *Fair Management*, p. 266.

6 Trustees' meeting, 17 May 1933, COP 3–19; Minutes of special meetings of Executive Committee, 10 January 1935, 3 July 1935, 4 March 1936, and 15 December 1937, COP 5–117; Lohr, *Fair Management*, p. 43.

7 Minutes of meeting of executive committee, 3 January 1935, COP 5–119; C. S. Peterson to California-Pacific International Exposition, 10 November 1934, COP 1–13114; unidentified newspaper clipping, 27 April 1938, COP 1–13117; J. Franklin Bell to F. C. Boggs, 21 May 1937.

8 *Chicago Tribune*, 7 March 1984; interview, Silas Fung, Haines City, Florida, 9 December 1992.

9 Edna Bobsin scrapbook, in author's possession.

10 *Chicago Tribune*, 3 June 1973.

11 *Chicago Tribune*, 25 May 1933; Heather Wright Lobdell, 'Keeping hope alive,' *Country Home*, XV, August 1993, pp. 34ff.

12 Paul Hutchinson, 'Progress on parade,' *Forum*, LXXXIX, June 1933, pp. 370–74; Robert McClory, *The Fall of the Fair: Communities Struggle for Fairness*, Chicago, 1986, pp. 1–38; *Chicago Tribune*, 21 June and 23 June 1985, 18 May and 3 December 1987.

13 Bruce Bliven, 'A century of treadmill,' *New Republic*, LXXVII, 15 November 1933, p. 13; *Chicago Tribune*, 28 October 1934.

Bibliography

Manuscript collections and other primary sources

World's Columbian Exposition

The records of this fair are incomplete; those that exist are scattered among various repositories. Some documents, including the records of the Board of Lady Managers, are at the Chicago Historical Society, while others are at the Art Institute in Chicago and the Chicago Public Library. Records pertinent to US government participation are housed at the Smithsonian Institution archives in Washington D.C. The Winterthur Museum and Library near Wilmington, Delaware, has an extensive collection of exhibitor brochures and catalogs from the exposition.

Contemporary published works abound. Two of the most important, written by participants, are Daniel H. Burnham and Francis D. Millet, *The World's Columbian Exposition: the Book of the Builders* (Chicago, 1894) and Burnham, *The Final Official Report of the Director of Works of the World's Columbian Exposition* (reprint edn, New York, 1989). Books such as Hubert Howe Bancroft, *The Book of the Fair* (Chicago, 1895), Henry Davenport Northrup and Nancy Hudson Banks, *The World's Fair as Seen in One Hundred Days* (New York, 1893), and Ben C. Truman, *History of the World's Fair* (Philadelphia, 1893), though highly adulatory, cover the fair and its attractions in great detail. In Henry Adams, *The Education of Henry Adams* (Boston, 1918) and William Dean Howells, 'Letters of an Altrurian Traveler,' serialized in *Cosmopolitan* magazine, two American literary giants indicate the impact the fair had on their thinking. Pictorial records of the fair include *Official Views of the World's Columbian Exposition Issued by the Department of Photography, C. D. Arnold, H. D. Higinbotham, Official Photographers* (Chicago, 1893), *The Dream City: A Portfolio of Photographic Views of the World's Columbian Exposition* (St Louis, 1893) and James W. Shepp and D. B. Shepp, *Shepp's World's Fair Photographed . . .* (Chicago, 1893).

Century of Progress Exposition

The records of this fair are housed in the Special Collections Department in the library of the University of Illinois at Chicago. Thoroughly indexed, they include reports, minutes of meetings, correspondence, legal and financial records, photographs, architectural renderings, and other material, including the relevant papers of Lenox Lohr and Rufus Dawes. The diaries of Daniel H. Burnham, Jr., and other Burnham family papers are in the library at the Art Institute, and an assortment of Century of Progress material, including many photographs, is located at the Chicago Historical Society. Records of federal government participation may be found at the National Archives in Washington D.C.

Contemporary accounts similar to those written about the World's Columbian Exposition do not exist for the Century of Progress, although Rufus C. Dawes, *Report of the President of a Century of Progress to the Board of Trustees* (Chicago, 1936) and Lenox R. Lohr, *Fair Management: The Story of a Century of Progress Exposition* (Chicago, 1952) are both important summaries of the fair's history by key participants. Basic descriptive information is found in the official guides to the fair, *Official Guide Book of the Fair* (Chicago, 1933, 1934) or in a more elaborate edition, *Official Guide and Time Saving Trips through the Fair* (Chicago, 1933). The Chicago newspapers, especially the *Chicago Tribune*, covered the fair on a daily basis and are also useful sources.

Books and articles

Abbott, Willis John, 'The makers of the fair,' *Outlook*, XLVII, 18 November 1893, pp. 884–85.

Adams, John Coleman, 'What a great city might be – a lesson from the White City,' *New England Magazine*, n.s., XIV, March 1896, pp. 3–13.

Adams, Mildred, 'America goes to the fair: 1893 and 1933,' *New York Times Sunday Magazine*, 17 September 1933.

Albert, Allen D., 'The architecture of the Chicago world's fair of 1933,' *American Architect*, CXXXV, 5 April 1929, pp. 421–30.

—, 'Chicago invites the world,' *Review of Reviews*, LXXXVII, May 1933, pp. 16–18.

'All roads lead to Chicago's Rainbow City,' *Literary Digest*, CXV, 3 June 1933, pp. 29–30ff.

Anderson, Norman D., *Ferris Wheels: An Illustrated History*, Bowling Green, Ohio, 1992.

'An engineer sees the world,' *Power Plant Engineering*, XXXVIII, June 1933, pp. 240–41.

Anonymous, *A Century of Nudity*, Chicago, 1933.

'Another great art exhibit for world's fair,' *Literary Digest*, CXVIII, 4 August 1934, p. 24.

Appelbaum, Stanley, *The Chicago World's Fair of 1893*, New York, 1980.

Art Institute of Chicago, *The Plan of Chicago: 1909–1979*, Chicago, 1979.

'Art of America is feature of Chicago's great 1934 exhibition,' *Art Digest*, VIII, June 1934, pp. 5–24.

'Aurora Borealis in the Westinghouse Century of Progress exhibit,' *Display World*, XII, May 1933, pp. 17, 25.

Bibliography

Aylesworth, Thomas G. and Virginia L. Aylesworth, *Chicago: The Glamour Years (1919–1941)*, New York, 1986.

Badger, Reid, *The Great American Fair: The World's Columbian Exposition and American Culture*, Chicago, 1979.

Barclay, George A., 'A Century of Progress International Exposition,' *Banker's Magazine*, CXXVII, July 1933, pp. 49–54.

—, 'Modern architecture dominates Century of Progress exposition,' *Architect and Engineer*, CXIII, June 1933, pp. 11–24.

Barrett, J. P., *Electricity at the Columbian Exposition*, Chicago, 1894.

Bell, J. Franklin, 'Applied science and industry at "A Century of Progress" exposition,' *Scientific Monthly*, XXXVI, March 1933, pp. 281–83.

Bickford, F. T., 'The government exhibit,' *Cosmopolitan*, XV, September 1893, pp. 603–6.

Bletter, Rosemarie Haag, 'The world of tomorrow: the future with a past,' in Elaine Koss (ed.), *High Styles: Twentieth Century American Design*, New York, 1986, pp. 84–127.

Bliven, Bruce, 'A century of treadmill,' *New Republic*, LXXVII, 15 November 1933, pp. 11–13.

'Branding the buildings at the Chicago fair,' *Literary Digest*, CXVI, 12 August 1933, p. 14.

Bulliet, Clarence J., 'A century of progress in collecting,' *Parnassus*, V, May 1933, pp. 1–7.

Burg, David F., *Chicago's White City of 1893*, Lexington, Ky., 1976.

Burnet, Mary Q., 'Indiana at the world's fair,' *American Magazine of Art*, XXVI, August 1933, p. 390.

Burnham, Daniel H., 'How Chicago finances its exposition,' *Review of Reviews*, LXXXVI, October 1932, pp. 37–38.

—, 'Skyscrapers of the future,' *Popular Mechanics*, LVIII, August 1932, pp. 177–79, 118A, 120A.

'Business and "the fair",' *Business Week*, 31 May 1933, pp. 11–14.

Cahan, Cathy and Richard Cahan, 'The lost city of the depression,' *Chicago History*, IV, Winter 1976–77, pp. 233–42.

Carskadon, T. R., 'Sally Rand dances to the rescue,' *American Mercury*, XXXV, July 1935, pp. 355–58.

Cawelti, John, 'America on display: the world's fairs of 1876, 1893, 1933,' in F. C. Jaher (ed.), *The Age of Industrialism in America*, New York, 1968, pp. 317–63.

'Century dairy exhibit on time,' *Milk Plant Monthly*, XXII, May 1933, pp. 51–52.

'Century of Progress, 1934,' World's Fair Supplement, *Chicago International Market*, Chicago, 1934, pp. 7–11, 32–38.

'Century of Progress exposition,' *The Painter's Magazine*, LIX, June 1932, pp. 8–10.

'Century of Progress paradox,' *Architectural Forum*, LXI, November 1934, pp. 374–79.

'Century's debt to castings,' *Foundry*, LXI, June 1933, pp. 22–26.

'Chemistry – economic dictator of the future,' *Power Plant Engineering*, XXXVIII, June 1933, pp. 252–55.

'Chicago exhibition,' *Saturday Review* (London), LXXVI, 11 November 1893, pp. 538–39.

'Chicago fair: exposition ends with riots and profits,' *Newsweek*, IV, 10 November 1934, p. 32.

'Chicago fair fire protection,' *Fire Protection*, XCVII, June 1932, p. 11.

'Chicago plan after fifteen years,' *Western Architect*, XXXV, January 1926, p. 2.

'Chicago's second world's fair,' *Review of Reviews*, LXXXVII, March 1933, pp. 38–39.

'Chicago world's fair: a Century of Progress,' *Commercial Art and Industry* (London), XIV, March 1933, pp. 99–100.

'Chrysler exhibition building,' *Architectural Forum*, LIX, December 1933, pp. 455–58.

Collier, Price, 'The foreign buildings,' *Cosmopolitan*, XV, September 1893, pp. 540–46.

Condit, Carl W., *Chicago, 1910–1929*, Chicago, 1973.

Corbett, Harvey Wiley, 'The architecture of the world's fair,' *Journal, Royal Architectural Institute of Canada*, XI, June 1934, pp. 100–2.

Cordato, Mary F., 'Representing the expansion of woman's sphere: women's work and culture at the world's fairs of 1876, 1893, and 1904,' unpublished Ph.D. dissertation, New York University, 1989.

Corn, Joseph and Brian Horrigan, *Yesterday's Tomorrows: Past Visions of the American Future*, New York, 1984.

Crissey, F., 'Why the Century of Progress architecture?,' *Saturday Evening Post*, CCV, 10 June 1933, pp. 16–17, 63–64.

Cromie, Robert, *A Short History of Chicago*, San Francisco, 1984.

Dacy, George, 'Uncle Sam's scientists display their contributions to progress at great world's fair,' *Popular Science Monthly*, CXXII, June 1933, pp. 9–11, 95.

Davis, Richard Harding, 'The last days of the fair,' *Harper's Weekly*, XXXVII, 21 October 1893, p. 1002.

Dawes, Rufus C., 'A Century of Progress adds a year,' *Literary Digest*, CXVII, 9 June 1934, p. 32.

Dean, Teresa H., *White City Chips*, Chicago, 1895.

Dedmon, Emmett, *Fabulous Chicago*, New York, 1953.

Dewey, Tom, *Art Nouveau, Art Deco, and Modernism: A Guide to the Styles, 1890–1940*, Jackson, Miss., 1983.

de Wit, Wim, 'Building an illusion: the design of the World's Columbian Exposition,' in Neil Harris *et al., Grand Illusion: Chicago's World's Fair of 1893*, Chicago, 1993.

Bibliography

'Display of fireworks at the Columbian Exposition,' *Scientific American*, LXIX, 2 December 1893, p. 359.

Downey, Dennis B., 'Rite of passage: the World's Columbian Exposition and American life,' unpublished Ph.D. dissertation, Marquette University, 1981.

Dredge, James, *A Scamper through the States*, London, 1893.

Duffus, R. L., 'The fair: a world of tomorrow,' *New York Times Sunday Magazine*, 28 May 1933.

Duis, Perry, *Chicago: Creating New Traditions*, Chicago, 1976.

Duncan, Alistair, *American Art Deco*, New York, 1986.

Dybwad, G. L. and Joy V. Bliss, *Annotated Bibliography: World's Columbian Exposition, Chicago, 1893*, Albuquerque, 1992.

'Electricity – the silent partner of industry,' *Power Plant Engineering*, XXXVIII, June 1933, pp. 256–59.

Evans, Almus Pratt, 'Exposition architecture: 1893 versus 1933,' *Parnassus*, V, May 1933, pp. 17–21.

Farrier, Clarence W., 'Exposition buildings unique in form and structure, *Engineering News-Record*, CX, 2 March 1933, pp. 278–82.

—, 'The gadgets: shelters, flags, decoration,' *Architectural Record*, LXXIII, 19 May 1933, pp. 363–65.

— and Bert M. Thorud, 'Design of the world's fair buildings,' *Western Society of Engineers*, XXXV, October 1930, pp. 384–94.

'Fate of the Chicago world's fair buildings,' *Scientific American*, LXXV, 3 October 1896, p. 267.

Findling, John and Kimberly D. Pelle (eds), *Historical Dictionary of World's Fairs and Expositions, 1851–1988*, Westport, Conn., 1990.

Flinn, John J., *Official Guide to Midway Plaisance . . .* , Chicago, 1893.

'Ford exposition at Chicago,' *Literary Digest*, CXVIII, 18 August 1934, p. 6.

'Forum of events,' *Architectural Record*, XXXIV, December 1933, p. 27.

Frankfurter, A. M., 'Architecture of a Century of Progress,' *Fine Arts*, XX, July 1933, pp. 5–11.

Friebe, Wolfgang, *Buildings of the World Exhibitions*, Leipzig, 1985.

Gilbert, James, *Perfect Cities: Chicago's Utopias of 1893*, Chicago, 1991.

'Government and the world's fair,' *Architectural Record*, II, January–March 1893, pp. 333–36.

Greif, Martin, *Depression Moderne: The Thirties Style in America*, New York, 1975.

Halstead, Murat, 'Electricity at the fair,' *Cosmopolitan*, XV, September 1893, pp. 577–83.

Hamilton, W., *The Time-Saver*, Chicago, 1893.

Harris, Neil, *Cultural Excursions: Marketing Appetites and Cultural Tastes in Modern America*, Chicago, 1990.

—, 'Memory and the White City,' in Neil Harris *et al., Grand Illusions: Chicago's World's Fair of 1893*, Chicago, 1993.

—, 'Museums, merchandising, and popular taste,' in Ian M. G. Quimby (ed.), *Material Culture and the Study of American Life*, New York, 1978.

Harshe, Robert B., 'The Century of Progress exhibition of fine arts,' *School Arts*, XXXIII, October 1933, pp. 76–80.

Haskell, Douglas, 'Mixed metaphors at Chicago,' *Architectural Review*, LXXIV, August 1933, pp. 47–49.

'Higher aspects of the Columbian Exposition,' *The Dial*, XIII, 1 November 1892, pp. 263–65.

Hillier, Bevis, *The Style of the Century: 1900–1980*, London, 1983.

Hines, Thomas S., *Burnham of Chicago: Architect and Planner*, New York, 1974.

Hirsch, Susan E. and Robert I. Goler, *A City Comes of Age: Chicago in the 1890s*, Chicago, 1990.

Holland, James P., 'Chicago and the world's fair,' *Chautauquan*, XVII, May 1893, pp. 136–39.

Holman, Charles T., 'Chicago fair to reopen in 1934,' *Christian Century*, L, 29 November 1933, p. 1513.

Holme, Bryan, 'Forceful architecture at Chicago's world's fair,' *Commercial Art and Industry*, XV, October 1933, pp. 136–42.

Holt, Barbara, 'An American dilemma on display: Black participation at the Chicago Century of Progress Exposition, 1933–34,' Report for the Chicago Urban League Research and Planning Department, n.d.

Horrigan, Brian, 'The home of tomorrow, 1927–1945,' in Joseph J. Corn (ed.), *Imagining Tomorrow: History, Technology, and the American Future*, Cambridge, Mass., 1986, pp. 137–63.

Huber, William, 'Story book playground for children,' *Highway Traveler*, IV, 1933, pp. 27, 42.

Hutchinson, Paul, 'Progress on parade,' *Forum*, LXXXIX, June 1933, pp. 370–74.

'Individual masterpieces,' *American Magazine of Art*, XXVI, June 1933, p. 279.

Inter-State Exposition Souvenir, Chicago, 1873.

Jailer, Mildred, 'Everybody loved a fair,' *Royle Forum*, CXLIII, 15 June 1973, pp. 2–4.

Jeffrey, Edward Turner, *Paris Universal Exposition, 1889*, n.p., 1889?

Jordy, William H., *American Architects and Their Buildings*, Volume III: Progressive and Academic Ideals at the Turn of the Twentieth Century, New York, 1972.

Kasson, John, *Amusing the Million: Coney Island at the Turn of the Century*, New York, 1978.

Keeler, Clinton, 'The White City and the Black City: the dream of civilization,' *American Quarterly*, II, Summer 1970, pp. 112–17.

Kihlstedt, Folke T., 'Utopia realized: the world's fairs of the 1930s,' in Joseph J. Corn (ed.), *Imagining Tomorrow: History, Technology, and the American Future*, Cambridge, Mass., 1986, pp. 97–118.

Bibliography

Kilham, Walter H., *Raymond Hood, Architect: Form Through Function in the American Skyscraper*, New York, 1973.

King, Rose G., 'Enchanted Island,' *Parents*, VIII, June 1933, pp. 31, 59–60.

Klaber, Eugene, 'World's fair architecture,' *American Magazine of Art*, XXVI, January 1933, pp. 292–98.

Knutson, Robert, 'The White City: the World's Columbian Exposition of 1893,' unpublished Ph.D. dissertation, Columbia University, 1956.

Kunz, George Frederick, 'Notes on industrial art in the Manufactures Building,' *Cosmopolitan*, XV, September 1893, pp. 547–59.

Laflin, Louis E., Jr., 'Fair-minded,' *Polity*, II, August 1934, pp. 169–90.

Lancaster, Clay, *The Incredible World's Parliament of Religions*, Fontwell, Sussex, 1987.

'Literary tributes to the world's fair,' *The Dial*, XV, 1 October 1893, pp. 176–78.

Littlewood, Thomas B., *Arch: A Promoter, Not a Poet: The Story of Arch Ward*, Ames, Iowa, 1990.

'Livestock and dairy industries feature of 1933 exposition,' *Rural Business*, III, November 1932, p. 10.

Lobdell, Heather Wright, 'Keeping hope alive,' *Country Home*, XV, August 1993, pp. 34, 43, 124.

Lohr, Lenox R., 'Chicago stages its second world's fair,' *Engineering News-Record*, CX, 2 March 1933, pp. 269–72.

Lowe, David, *Lost Chicago*, Boston, 1975.

Lundberg, Bengt Theodor, 'Arts and crafts at the Swedish Chicago exposition, 1933,' (pamphlet), n.p., 1933.

Lynes, Russell, *The Lively Audience*, New York, 1985.

Magee, H. W., 'Building with light,' *Popular Mechanics*, LVIII, July 1932, pp. 8–14.

—, 'The enchanted island,' *Popular Mechanics*, LIX, February 1933, pp. 202–16.

Maher, George W., 'The restoration of the Fine Arts Building of the world's fair,' *Architectural Forum*, XXXV, July 1921, pp. 35–37.

Mayer, Harold M. and Richard C. Wade, *Chicago: Growth of a Metropolis*, Chicago, 1969.

Mayer, Milton S., 'To the brave belongs the fair,' *Vanity Fair*, XXX, April 1933, pp. 17–20, 60.

McClory, Robert, *The Fall of the Fair: Communities Struggle for Fairness*, Chicago, 1986.

McConnell, J. L., 'Lighting heads the list of special facilities,' *Engineering News-Record*, CX, 2 March 1933, pp. 283–85.

McKenna, Ruth, *Chicago: These First Hundred Years*, Chicago, 1933.

[McLean, Robert Craik], 'The Chicago Plan after fifteen years,' *Western Architect*, XXXV, January 1926, p. 1.

Meier, August and Elliott M. Rudwick, 'Negro protest at the Chicago world's fair, 1933–1934,' *Journal of the Illinois State Historical Society*, LIX, Summer 1966, pp. 161–71.

Meikle, Jeffrey, *Twentieth Century Limited: Industrial Design in America, 1925–1939*, Philadelphia, 1979.

'A midway review,' *The Dial*, XV, 1 September 1893, pp. 105–7.

Miller, Donald L., 'The White City,' *American Heritage*, XLIV, July–August 1993, pp. 71–87.

Mitchell, Edmund, 'International effects of the fair,' *Engineering Magazine*, VI, January 1894, pp. 468–72.

Moore, Charles, *Daniel H. Burnham: Architect, Planner of Cities*, Boston, 1921.

Muccigrosso, Robert, *Celebrating the New World: Chicago's Columbian Exposition of 1893*, Chicago, 1993.

N. H. D., 'Columbian expectoration,' [Correspondence] *Nation*, LVII, 2 November 1893, p. 328.

National Museum of American Art, *Revisiting the White City: American Art at the 1893 World's Fair*, Washington D.C., 1993.

Neufeld, Maurice, 'The White City: the beginnings of a planned civilization in America,' *Journal of the Illinois State Historical Society*, XXVII, April 1934, pp. 71–93.

Niles, Barbara, 'Century of Progress,' *Design*, XXXIV, July 1932, p. 68.

Norton, Charles B., *World's Fairs from London 1851 to Chicago 1893*, Chicago, 1890.

'Now it's let's go – to Chicago,' *National Magazine*, LXI, May–June 1933, pp. 41–45.

Olmsted, Frederick Law, 'The landscape architecture of the World's Columbian Exposition,' *Inland Architect*, XXII, September 1893, p. 19.

Owings, Nathaniel, 'Amusement features of the exposition,' *Architectural Record*, LXXIII, May 1933, pp. 355–62.

—, 'New materials and building methods for Chicago exposition,' *Architectural Record*, LXXI, April 1932, pp. 279–88ff.

—, *The Spaces in Between: An Architect's Journey*, Boston, 1973.

Partridge, William O., 'The educational value of world's fairs,' *Forum*, XXXIII, March 1902, pp. 121–26.

Payant, Felix, 'The editor's page,' *Design*, XXXV, October 1933, p. 1.

'Permanent impress of the Chicago fair,' *Literary Digest*, CXVI, 25 November 1933, p. 29.

Phillips, John W., 'A Century of Progress,' unpublished senior research thesis, Wharton School of Finance and Commerce, 1934.

'Physics – modern genie of the lamp,' *Power Plant Engineering*, XXXVIII, June 1933, pp. 248–51.

Pierce, Bessie L., *A History of Chicago*, 3 vols, Chicago, 1937–57.

'The queen of the sciences,' *Power Plant Engineering*, XXXVIII, June 1933, pp. 246–47.

Raley, Dorothy (ed.), *A Century of Progress Homes and Furnishings*, Chicago, 1934.

Randolph, Robert I., 'Call victory 1933,' *American Legion Monthly* XIV, February 1933, pp. 22–23, 40–41.

Bibliography

Rogers, Joseph M., 'Lessons from international exhibitions,' *Forum*, XXXII, November 1901, pp. 500–10.

Ryan, W. D'Arcy, 'Lighting a Century of Progress,' *Electrical Engineering*, LIII, May 1934, pp. 731–36.

—, 'Lighting an exposition,' *Electrical World*, CI, 1932, pp. 687–88, 697–98.

Rydell, Robert, *All the World's a Fair: Visions of Empire at American International Expositions, 1876–1916*, Chicago, 1984.

— (ed.), *Books of the Fairs*, Washington D.C., 1992.

—, 'The culture of imperial abundance,' in Simon J. Bronner (ed.), *Consuming Visions: Accumulation and Display of Goods in America, 1880–1920*, New York, 1989.

—, 'The fan dance of science,' *Isis*, LXXVI, 1985, pp. 525–42.

—, *World of Fairs: The Century-of-Progress Expositions*, Chicago, 1994.

Sandweiss, Eric, 'Around the world in a day,' *Illinois Historical Journal*, LXXXIV, Spring 1991, pp. 2–14.

Sawyers, June Skinner, *Chicago Portraits*, Chicago, 1991.

Schlereth, Thomas J., *Cultural History and Material Culture*, Charlottesville, Va., 1990.

—, *Victorian America: Transformations in Everyday Life, 1876–1915*, New York, 1991.

Schuyler, Montgomery, 'Last words about the world's fair,' *Architectural Record*, III, January–March 1894, p. 292.

—, 'State buildings at the world's fair,' *Architectural Record*, III, July–September 1893, pp. 55–71.

'Science at the Century of Progress exposition in 1934,' *Scientific Monthly*, XXXIX, November 1934, pp. 475–78.

Segal, Howard P., *Technological Utopianism in American Culture*,Chicago, 1985.

—, 'Utopian fairs,' *Chicago History*, XII, 1983, pp. 7–9.

Sharp, Robert V. (ed.), *Constructing the Fair: Platinum Photographs by C. D. Arnold of the World's Columbian Exposition*, Chicago, 1992.

Shaw, Marian, *World's Fair Notes: a Woman Journalist Views Chicago's Columbian Exposition*, reprint edn, St Paul, Minn., 1992.

'Significance of the Century of Progress art exhibition,' *Bulletin of the Art Institute of Chicago*, XXVII, September 1933, pp. 81–89.

Skidmore, Louis, 'The architecture of the Century of Progress,' *Display World*, XII, May 1933, pp. 10–15, 32.

—, 'The Hall of Science, a Century of Progress Exposition: details of structure and equipment,' *Architectural Forum*, LVII, October 1932, pp. 361–66.

—, 'Planning the exposition displays,' *Architectural Record*, LXXIII, 19 May 1933, pp. 342–74.

Skramstad, Harold K., Jr., 'Interpreting material culture: a view from the other side of the glass,' in Ian M. G. Quimby (ed.), *Material Culture and the Study of American Life*, New York, 1978, pp. 175–200.

Slade, Thomas M., 'The "Crystal House" of 1934,' *Journal of the Society of Architectural Historians*, XXIX, December 1970, pp. 350–53.

Smith, Henry Justin, *Chicago's Great Century, 1833–1933*, Chicago, 1933.

Smith, Howard R., 'Six months to go,' *Commerce*, XXIX, December 1932, pp. 18–20, 36ff.

Snider, Denton J., *World's Fair Studies*, Chicago, 1895.

Stern, Rudi, *The New Let There Be Neon*, New York, 1988.

Stuart, William H., *The Twenty Incredible Years*, Chicago, 1935.

Susman, Warren I., 'The people's fair: contradictions of a consumer society,' in Warren I. Susman (ed.), *Culture as History*, New York, 1984.

—, 'Ritual fairs,' *Chicago History*, XII, 1983, pp. 4–7.

Teegen, Otto, 'Painting the exposition buildings,' *Architectural Record*, LXXIII, May 1933, pp. 366–69.

'Three-day tour of the world's fair,' *Santa Fe Magazine*, XXIX, September 1934, pp. 33–38.

'Thumb tacks and T-square,' *Architect and Engineer*, CXV, October 1933, p. 4.

Tozer, Lowell, 'American attitudes toward machine technology, 1893–1933,' unpublished Ph.D. dissertation, University of Minnesota, 1953.

'United States Department of Labor at the Century of Progress Exposition, Chicago, 1933,' *Monthly Labor Review*, XXXVI, 1933, pp. 1087–88.

Van Zandt, J. Parker, 'A miracle in cans,' *Review of Reviews and World's Work*, XC, October 1934, pp. 54–57.

— and L. Rohe Walter, 'King customer at a Century of Progress,' *Review of Reviews*, XC, September 1934, pp. 22–27.

Van Zanten, David, 'The nineteenth century: the projecting of Chicago as a commercial city and the rationalization of design and construction,' in Art Institute of Chicago, *Chicago and New York: Architectural Interactions*, Chicago, 1984.

Vogelsgesang, Shepard, 'Color treatment of exhibit space,' *Architectural Record*, XXXIII, May 1933, pp. 370–74.

Walter, L. Rohe, 'Look homeward, America!,' *Review of Reviews and World's Work*, XC, October 1934, pp. 27–30.

Warner, Charles Dudley, 'The last day of the fair,' *Harper's Weekly*, XXXVII, 11 November 1893, pp. 1074–75.

Watson, Dudley C., 'What Chicago learned,' *American Magazine of Art*, XXVII, February 1934, pp. 77–79.

Weber, Eva, *Art Deco in America*, New York, 1985.

Weimann, Jeanne Madeline, *The Fair Women*, Chicago, 1981.

'Weird lights at Chicago fair,' *Literary Digest*, CXV, 25 March 1933, p. 32.

'Welding in the Ford building at the 1934 Century of Progress,' *Architectural Record*, LXXV, June 1934, p. 467.

White, Theo B., *Paul Philippe Cret: Architect and Teacher*, Philadelphia, 1973.

Williams, Kenny J., *In the City of Men: Another Story of Chicago*, Nashville, Tenn., 1974.

Bibliography

Willoughby, Raymond, 'Building tells the story of progress,' *Nation's Business*, XXI, June 1933, pp. 22–24.

Willy, John, 'Impressions of the 1934 world's fair,' *Hotel Monthly*, XLII, September 1934, pp. 22–24.

Woltersdorf, Arthur F., 'Carnival architecture,' *American Architect*, CXLIII, July 1933, pp. 10–21.

Woollcott, Alexander, 'Shouts and murmurs,' *New Yorker*, 15 July 1933, pp. 26, 28.

Young, Hugh E., 'Lakefront boulevard link forms milestone in Chicago plan,' *Engineering News-Record*, CXVIII, 15 April 1937, pp. 546–48.

Zukowsky, John (ed.), *Chicago Architecture, 1872–1922*, Munich, 1987.

Index

Page numbers in **bold** refer to illustrations.

167

Index

Index

Index